A RELIGION AGAINST ITSELF

A Religion
Against Itself

ROBERT W. JENSON

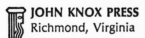 **JOHN KNOX PRESS**
Richmond, Virginia

Library of Congress Catalog Card Number: 67-12427
© M. E. Bratcher 1967
Printed in the United States of America
24-0690-WB-2027

First printing April 1967
Second printing June 1967

To my father and father-in-law,
whose teaching and example—in
the one instance by way of my
wife—are deeply responsible
for the contents of this book,
though they probably will never admit it.

PREFACE

Since footnotes have been eliminated, let me acknowledge my indebtedness in advance. In this book, I owe the most to: Karl Barth, Dietrich Bonhoeffer, Peter Brunner, Gerhard Ebeling, Mircea Eliade, and C. B. Martin (listing in alphabetical order). I am aware that each of them will be astonished to find himself on the same list with the others. I can only say that I do not believe myself indebted by way of an eclectic attempt at combination, but by way of help in understanding found when needed. Those who know these men will see where my indebtedness approaches actual borrowing.

Let me also thank Professor John Bale and my wife, who read and improved the manuscript, and Constance Kronlokken, my secretary.

Some material in Chapters II and IV appeared earlier in *dialog* magazine.

Fifth after Trinity, 1966

CONTENTS

I. THE REBELLION AGAINST RELIGION

There seem to be more and more of us—Christians repelled by our own religion. There seem to be more and more who believe in Christ and wish there were some way of believing other than being religious, who precisely for the sake of Christ long to overcome religiosity. We have no way of knowing whether this is the onset of a disease or the beginning of a recovery, whether it is a curse or a blessing. We can only try to work out the logic and the music of our condition, in the hope that in so doing we may be of some help to the church and perhaps also to those touched and puzzled by the church. For the task of the church is to make sense of the gospel, of the story of Jesus as the Christ. Surely, therefore, what we say and experience in trying to make sense of the gospel to ourselves must be of some use to the community, even should our condition prove aberrant.

We hope, of course, that our thinking will provide more than an instructive error. No one can help seeing the world and the human story refracted by his own passions and anxieties. Thus the worldliness we experience in ourselves seems to us to offer an interpretation of the present situation of our civilization and of the particular task laid on those who would tell the gospel in that situation. Here is the origin of slogans about our world like "post-Christian," "post-religious," or "atheistic," and of slogans that specify the needed form of the gospel as "religionless" or "secular."

Much of this sloganeering has been amateurish and some of it destructive. The great fuss just recently about "believing in the death of God" was both. Even if we could make sense of the

notion of the death of God, if faith in Christ kills God then
surely it is Christ we believe in and not this remarkable supernatural by-product.

Nevertheless, the malaise all this sloganeering expresses is
real enough. The time has come, however, for more than howls
of anguish or of glee. The time has come to be serious. Those
of us who believe that it is for the sake of Jesus Christ—indeed,
for the sake of the *God* who is revealed in Christ—that rebellion
against religion is to be justified, if at all, must get on with the
work of Christian theology. It is time to try to let the gospel tell
us what then we shall do and say, if we are not to be religious.
Indeed, I confess at the beginning that whatever radicalism my
thought may possess is at least intended to be simply the radicalism of the great tradition of Christian theology.

Perhaps an interpretation of the world and of the gospel's
address to the world, made from the standpoint of the distrust
of religion, will, on that day when each believer's work is assayed,
be judged wrong. In the meantime, let us get on with it. What
would antireligious faith look like?

The Changing Gospel

It is worth repeating that it is an interpretation of our time
that we are working with. In some grand way, it seems to make
obvious sense to speak of "modern man" or "the contemporary
world-view," and I propose to do so. Yet it is always easy to
debunk such language. Any proposed description of what "modern man" is like, perhaps that he cannot understand "myths" or
cannot believe in "supernatural beings," can be immediately
and crushingly countered by pointing to groups or whole populations of whom these statements are not true, or even by simply
saying, "I believe in supernatural entities and I am just as
contemporary as you." All one can say in reply is that such
refutations are in a way irrelevant—that an interpretation is
offered and not the results of a survey, that "modern man" means
"my fellows and myself considered in those sides of our lives
that I find most important for understanding our hopes and
problems."

Thus suppose we say that a worldly culture is one that does not, in its customs, laws, or creative arts, reckon seriously with supernatural realities. And suppose we claim that our culture is worldly in this sense. What exactly are we asserting? It would be folly to assert that no one in our culture talks seriously of the God of theism, or that prayer is no longer used as medicine, or that ideological gods and demons, such as "Americanism" or "Communism," do not flourish in the land. Clearly all these things are very much around. Indeed, it is probable that no culture can ever do wholly without supernaturalism. What we can and do claim is that our supernaturalism is false, that it is not a spring of thought and action but rather a screen to hide the true springs thereof.

Thus to say that we have a worldly culture is to evaluate one aspect—the religion—of that culture. It is to take up—at second-hand—a strain of prophetic judgment: "I hate, I despise your feasts, and I take no delight in your solemn assemblies." More in our mode: "Your religion is phony!" How can we support such an evaluation? Dare we end as Amos did, ". . . says the Lord . . ."? We dare, I think, just that. All Christian theology is done in the faith that the Lord has indeed spoken, that the story of Jesus of Nazareth is his word. The prophets and the sons of the prophets always had to interpret the oracle—and it was possible to err. Our judgment upon the religion of our time is an attempt to interpret that religion by the story of Jesus. We may be reading the story of Jesus wrongly. But in that story the Lord has spoken, and it is our responsibility to say what we believe we have heard, to take the risk of ". . . says the Lord." That we have heard rightly is supported or not by the success or failure of the whole interpretation. Indeed, the final criterion can only be his judgment whose word we presume to interpret, can only be the *last* judgment.

However, a less grandiose support for calling our supernaturalism fraudulent is, at this beginning of our conversation, perhaps more appropriate. Then one has to appeal to the court of the intestines. The religious mimicry of our congregations, the rhetoric of our denominations, the theologies of our Sunday schools, the pseudo-divine personifications of our economic ideologies together with the bloody war-liturgies of their worship, the Sunday-morning-radio "spark of the divine in every man," Sallman's Jesus, and "My God and I" share one common feature: they all make one sick, and in exactly the same way that celluloid carnations and "lifetime" Christmas trees make one sick. They are unmistakably phony.

I do not attack the religion of our culture for the sake of some other, better, perhaps genuine, supernaturalism. Nor is this a negative verdict on our culture as such. Rather, it is but part of an attempt to discern what is distinctive about contemporary culture, an attempt which labels our culture "worldly," i.e., lacking a true supernaturalism. It is part of an interpretation of the human story and of our particular segment thereof, an interpretation which sees the replacement of genuine supernaturalism by false supernaturalism as a very specific epoch in the history of our culture.

Moreover, I interpret this epoch as one which believers should greet gladly as a specific new opportunity for the telling of the gospel. The cry "Down with religion" is probably never evoked except by false and unworthy religion. But the cry, once triggered, is a revolt against religion as such, against a whole previous form of human existence, whether in genuine or bogus manifestations. And to that revolt the believer can, I am convinced, respond. This is the project of this book.

To see what I mean by the believer's response to such a cultural epoch requires some very general reflections. The gospel, since it is the story of a man, is not a timeless truth discoverable at any time by reflection or observation. Only by tradition does this story live, only as one man has told another and he a third and so on from "those who first believed" to us. Through the centuries, this tradition has traversed many epochs of culture and may yet traverse many others. The branch of the tradition which leads to us carried the gospel from Semites to Greeks, then conquered the Latins. It cooperated with the remnants of antique tradition to create Christendom. It then survived the collapse of Christendom—indeed, in the Reformation, took that collapse as occasion to blaze momentarily with new purity and vigor.

The gospel is narrative of what happened with Jesus, spoken with the claim that this story tells the final destiny also of those who hear it told. "What will finally come of your life," it says, "is to be discovered in the story of this man." Therefore the gospel is, and must be, always told in the language in which those who hear seek to understand their own destinies—which means those who at any period are *then* there to hear. The gospel has spoken to Jews of judgment, to Greeks of participation in divinity, to Latins of the new law, to feudal societies of merit, and to the protomoderns of the Reformation of the overcoming of anxiety and absurdity. Every epoch of the gospel's journey through man's history has produced a new version of the gospel. The Greeks made of it a theology, the Latins made of it a government, the Middle Ages made of it a ladder on which to mount a feudal hierarchy of being, and Luther made of it a word to the tormented conscience.

Is not the gospel perverted in all these transformations? Of course. But this says only that the handing on of the gospel from one man to another is a part of human history and shares in its ambiguity—all growth is also decay, and moth and rust do indeed corrupt anything that takes time. Throughout the history of the church there have been those who have called the church to return to an original purity, and they have always had good reason. Yet only those of them have been effective who have also, whether they knew it or not, called the church forward across an epoch of history into some new transformation of its message. The gospel's place is history, and perversion is simply one of the constant conditions of its life. The other side of the transformation of the gospel in history is far more important: each new epoch of history presents the preachers of the gospel with a new opportunity.

Each new epoch of history gives the bearers of the gospel tradition the opportunity to discover and be captured by some side of the gospel hitherto implicit. Thus there is indeed such a thing as being freed by the gospel to creative philosophical reflection—but it took the Greeks to discover it. So also the Latins quite rightly discerned what the Greeks tended to over-look, that the gospel is an existential word about the problems and decisions of earthly life. Now, it is the hope and contention of the worldly among the believers that the great secularism of the contemporary world is our opportunity to discover a true worldliness of the gospel. For my own part, at any rate, this hope is sustained by the conviction that nothing can happen in history uncongenial to the gospel. For the gospel purports to be about the end of the human story. If it is true, then all that the inexhaustible newness and unpredictability of time can create can but cooperate in elucidating the possibilities of the gospel.

Religion

It is time to say just what it is we wish to be free of, what this "religion" is that is claimed to be antiquated in history, and by being antiquated to give the gospel the chance for a new explication. I hesitate here. It is both easier and more appropriate to *use* the word "religion" than to define it. Certainly no blatant definition of terms should be attempted. Nevertheless, I do have to indicate by rough pointings and descriptions whose cat is being belled.

Religion is one way of dealing with the question: "What am I for? What will come of me?" It is easy enough to analyze this question, interpreted as a request for information, as meaningless. But the question will not down. Why not?

The question arises only for men, only for us odd beings who experience ourselves not as things but as stories. When I try to understand and evaluate myself, the "self" I have to work on is my past history. I trace out the dramatic coherence of a sequence in time of events, which I identify as together the happenings of *my* life precisely by this dramatic coherence. I am a plot.

We experience ourselves as stories. But we also experience ourselves as unfinished stories. It is the last act, the catastrophe and denouement, of a drama which makes sense of the whole series of enacted occurrences, which makes of them a coherent whole so as to be a plot, a story, at all. Only, therefore, from its end can I grasp my life as my true self, as a meaningful whole. Thus not until I die can I know what my life is about, what its plot is, what or who I am. But then it is too late. This is the agony of mortality: I cannot achieve myself, I cannot live to any purpose, I cannot justify my actions, except by dying.

Each of us lives his life as the hero of a drama missing its last act, its denouement. This is why "What am I here for?" always remains an open question. And it is just because it always remains an open question that we cannot cease to ask it, that the reason for living comes up as a question and not as a self-evidency. To live, to grasp and evaluate myself—i.e., to choose and plan and hope and despair and dream—is something that I as a mortal can do only by questioning my life, by doubting my worth, by asking after myself.

Religion is one way of dealing with this question—many will say the only way. Religion is living in the hope that perhaps the last act is not missing after all. It is living in the hope that somewhere in what is already done and in what I already am, somewhere in what is now available to me, what I am for is already there. Religion is the hope that somewhere the last act of my life is already in rehearsal and that I can watch. Religion is thus the lived refusal to take death seriously; it is the struggle against time. Religion is the discovery—or invention—of eternity.

Religion is life in the confidence that in the repertoire of acts which the story of man to date presents there are some that, if we perform them, will guarantee our destiny: rituals, or deeds of love, or prayers, or fastings, or political activisms, or what will you. Or that there are, of the proposed answers to the question of what is to be accomplished by our lives, some that can be discovered to be correct—and then perhaps the required act is that we "believe" these hard enough. Or that some of the objects of our experience, if contemplated, will mirror to us the state of our fulfillment.

Such a life creates a world "above"—or "beyond" or "at the depth of"—the world of our daily stories and of the death which terminates them. For if the conclusion of our play, hidden as we play our temporal stories in the impenetrable future of death, is nevertheless already enacted, then it can only be enacted in something like the mind of an author, standing above the play and holding what in the play are past and future in a superior present, in the "all-at-once-now" of eternity. In this world of time, the fulfillment of our lives is exactly what is not yet enacted. Religion creates a supernatural reality, a stage where the same drama is performed as on this one, but in its completed version.

Some religions reflect on what they do, and think our supernaturalist metaphysics; others do not. It is the way of living that is important. It is not the dream of an eternally perfected reality that is in itself religion. Religion is *using* that dream. It is a life which seizes the supernatural eternal presence of what is in time beyond our grasp, and in this way guarantees its own meaning and fulfillment. So also the other world of religion is not really "transcendent." On the contrary, it must be open to us, there must be acts that lead into it, reliable knowledge of what it is like, places in this world that let us see into it.

Thus the most familiar phenomena of religion are the gods. For the gods transcend the division of past, present, and future; they are eternal (though not necessarily in the sophisticated sense that philosophy works out). They are the presence of the future: insofar as I have to do with them, I already have to do with custodians of my last fate, or, as in the case of the Greek gods, with the embodiments of my ideal perfection. They are also past: stories can be told of them, and their nature and character is therefore knowable. I can reckon with them, predict their actions, control my relation to them. The destiny they mediate is cognitively and actively mine. Thus concourse with the gods means possession now of the future fulfillment, the meaning, of life. The function of the gods is to justify me.

Yet familiar as the gods are, religion can dispense with them. Indeed, it seems to get along best when it has done so, as in Buddhism (so that one may suspect that attempts to be Christian without God do not overcome religion but rather capitulate to it). Even the palest gods remain, after all, somewhat distinct from me and so inconveniently uncontrollable. All that religion really requires is that there be *something* that is a special, different kind of reality to which we can repair to escape time. A few examples from Christianity might be: the book whose narrations are not subject to historical critique and whose "truths" never need interpretation as time moves on from the time of its writing; "saving history," as the stretch of history somehow of a different kind than all others; special areas of life held inaccessible to ordinary explanation and manipulation and preserved for religion, the "inner life" or "border situations"; or "religious experience" as a special kind of experience.

To live with my "important" acts, thoughts, and apprehensions distinguished in this way from the rest of my temporal story, which ends in death and therefore lacks a fulfillment, and by so living to be sure that my life has some point, is to be religious. If someone wants to say that by "religion" he means something altogether different, let him do so. We have no dispute (unless having, let us say, established the viability of what he means by "religion," he slips in an equivocation which results in apparent conclusions about "religion" as used here).

Of religion in this sense I claim that it is dead, or that where it seems to survive it is as a cover-up for the true and living motivations and dreams of our lives. The way for someone to dispute this evaluation will be for him to *live* a religion which is not fraudulent.

We may ask if there is any explanation for the death of religion. I think there is. The dominant cultural forces of our age are incompatible with genuine religion. We will discuss two: natural science and the historical attitude.

The war between science and religion is generally supposed to be over. So it is, but only because science is a decisive winner. Religion has retired from the field. By science, I do not mean the current body of scientific results; I mean the human activity of *doing* science. When it is argued that the conflict between religion and specific results of science was never necessary and is anyway now over, this may be so—which is not to say it will not start up again. But science and religion as ways of living are irreconcilable.

How so? There are several ways of getting at this. One that fits our present thought is simply to note that the maxim of scientific practice is "Wait and see," whereas religion counsels "Seize it now." A scientific hypothesis *is* an opinion held pending further evidence. We say, for example, "If it is true that to every action an opposed reaction corresponds, then when I press this lever that pointer will move to the left." Then we press the lever and look. The truth or falsity of a scientific assertion is always something we leave to the future to determine. Nor is this simply one characteristic among others. It is precisely because an assertion is held permanently open to confirmation or disconfirmation by events that it is a scientific assertion instead of some other kind of assertion, perhaps mythical or mathematical.

One who lives his life consistently after the maxim of science cannot, therefore, also be religious. For religion is exactly identifying some part of reality where the future is already realized, where nothing, therefore, can be permitted to change: where "Wait and see" is blasphemous.

To be religious, there must be some objects of my experience with which I refuse to follow the scientific maxim. Perhaps the events narrated in the Bible must not be investigated critically and historically. Or grandmother's recovery after prayer must be immune to medical explanation: "The doctors had given her up." Or religious experience must not be psychologically or sociologically tampered with.

In an unscientific culture this is no problem. In a scientific culture we can achieve it by compartmentalizing our lives: by being religious some days about some things and scientific other days about other things. Compartmentalizing is not, of course, always the worst policy. Perfect unity of all sides and events of our lives is what we await from heaven, and in the meantime we have to deal with our inconsistencies somehow. But compartmentalizing will not work for religion. For religion is supposed to provide exactly the unity of our stories, the denouement which reveals their coherence. Compartmentalized "Sunday religion" is, as the preachers have always said, a contradiction. The necessity of compartmentalizing religion to preserve it at all in a society whose behavior is dominated by the maxim of science is the origin of the fraudulence of contemporary religion. Religion survives only as a performance which is in fact irrelevant to most of the rest of what we think and do. Yet it must pretend to be the guide and motivation of all that we think and do. It survives, necessarily, only as a pretense.

When the scientific policy of being deliberately noncommittal turns from nature to our own past, the modern attitude to history is born. The impact of this on our lives is probably even greater than that of the natural sciences. For we study the past and recount to ourselves the stories of how men have lived in order to search out if we can the plot of human life, in order to discover how *we* should live. Nor is this merely one among several ways of researching our roles in life. The past is our only repertoire of possible hopes, beliefs, and choices. All specifically human life, all choosing, planning, believing, creating, takes place as culture, i.e., by grace of the inheritance of the past. From the past we receive the intellectual, religious, political, and artistic traditions which are our humanity. Or, in one formula, from the past we receive language. To be human is to speak. And to learn to speak is to learn from those who have spoken before.

It is, therefore, a momentous step to adapt the noncommittal attitude of science to the tradition of the past by which we live, to say, "I know that's what tradition *says* happened. Now what *really* happened?" For thereby we make a break between ourselves and the past which lives in our tradition and by which we live. We step back and look at it in a cool and detached fashion. Then we become aware that Socrates and Charlemagne and Luther and grandpa, from whose creations of language and custom we live and will continue to live, are nevertheless different from and separated from us. We become aware, that is, of time. We do not therefore cease to live from the past. Rather, we live from what we now see to be a story in time. We become aware of the essential temporality of human life. Therewith it is all up with religion, which is the conviction of the essential eternity of human life.

Which came first, the scientific habit or the apprehension of human life as history, is unimportant. My exposition perhaps makes it appear that the scientific habit produces the historical habit. But that is only because I picked up that end of the stick. It could just as well have been done the other way around. What is important is that we have got both habits, and that both are incompatible with religion.

Faith Versus Religion

Our question is: Are the modern habits of life incompatible also with faith in Christ? I have asserted that they are not, that on the contrary faith can and should find in the birth of a worldly culture the opportunity to proclaim itself more directly and unambiguously than ever. It is the burden of the whole book to make this plausible by showing how it might be done, but already here at the beginning it is probably necessary to show at least some indications of compatibility between the gospel and worldliness. In order to be sure our examples of gospel are authentic, we will use some biblical texts.

The very beginning of the Bible is an audacious piece of religion-debunking. We lift just one verse from the long polemic which is Genesis 1: "And God made the two great lights . . . he made the stars also. And God set them in the firmament of the heavens to give light upon the earth." What is the point of this? Ancient man found his greatest single religious assurance—later, his greatest religious anxiety—in the sight of the wheeling heavenly beings. There were his gods, visibly enclosing him, knowable and predictable in their visibility and eternal in the mathematics of their behavior. The words of the cynical old priest who wrote our passage were a deliberate impiety: "Gods nothing! Energy sources that God hung up there!" From here to Galileo is a matter of details.

What is the gospel in this? Quite simply: "You do not need to fear and worship the world in which God has put you, or any part of it. Subdue it, have dominion over it—enjoy it!" The first chapter of the Bible is like the last, where we read: "And when I heard and saw [these things], I fell down to worship at the feet of the angel who showed them to me; but he said to me, 'You must not do that! I am a fellow servant with you . . . Worship God.' "

In between, the message is the same. Christ was crucified for blasphemy. Paul, who understood the crucifixion better than most, spent most of his literary energy in antireligious polemic. For example, he wrote to the believers at Galatia: "You observe days, and months, and seasons, and years! I am afraid I have labored over you in vain." What was the matter with days and months and seasons and years? Surely we can, also in our life of faith, not do without a calendar? But the Galatians "observed" the calendar, i.e., they *watched* it, *expecting* something from it. What could be expected from a calendar? Eternity—for the great feasts and fasts of a religious calendar return each year with the same content. Every great festival cancels time, for each year despite all that has happened we end where we began.

What is the gospel in Paul's polemic? "You do not need to cling to the past, to the way things have always been. If something utterly new should happen, something which broke the sheltering wheel of the returning seasons and festivals, you need not fear. You may take the risk of the future. For the risk of the future has been made by Jesus Christ to be the kind of risk which love brings."

Religion comforts and sustains us by abolishing the radical newness and unpredictability of the future, by suspending the future into an eternal present. There is, trusts religion, something already there that guarantees the future, guarantees that something good will come of me. Because this something is already there it is knowable, and because it is knowable I can experience the guarantee of my future which it gives. To be already present and knowable, it must be given in the past—in the "once-upon-a-time" of mythical stories about how things are in eternity, or in the "I fast twice in the week" record of accomplishments at which legalistic religion looks back. Religion is the rule of the past. The security it gives is that all will be again as it was, the security of return to the womb, of peace in death. This religious security is exactly what the gospel seeks to free us from.

The gospel too speaks of a past (see the "has been" in the last paragraph but one): it narrates what happened with Jesus of Nazareth. But religion speaks of the past as the perfected state to which we are called to return. The past which the gospel narrates is quite different. As a past event, Jesus' life was not at all an eternally perfected, and in this way past, ideal state of affairs. What happened with Jesus was a temporal event like any other human life, and therefore essentially unfinished, unaccomplished, dependent on the future for its completion. Jesus ended, as we all do, in death, the remorseless and unanswerable challenge to all claims to have achieved fulfillment and completion. As an item of the past, Jesus is not perfected, not ideal. We are not called to return to him. Only as he rose—i.e., only as he became the one we await from the future—is the past Jesus our destined fulfillment.

The gospel denies the holiness of the status quo, of what we are and have done, or even could conceivably have been or have done. To affirm the story of the Crucified is to renounce religion's eternity in which all is already really accomplished. When we then also say "He is risen," part of what we say is that we will await the unknown and unexpected future eagerly and with anticipation. Faith means living by waiting, living by hope for a time beyond eternity.

Religion ties the future to the past in an eternal, static present. The gospel ties the past to the future to make of the present the moment of choice and decision, the moment of change.

The antireligious polemic of the Bible is, therefore, polemic in principle. This is not a mere matter of competition between religions (as to that, religions in their normal state are not competitive). Yet neither is the polemic conducted on behalf of blank absence of concern for the question to which religion responds. The gods are attacked for the sake of God.

Is then the faith of the Bible after all about a god and therefore itself a sort of religion? To be sure—but it is a religion opposed to religion. Faith as we see it in Scripture is religion at odds with itself, a religion polemic against its own character as a religion. What could this be like? The opportunity to answer this particular question about itself is the specific opportunity given faith by modern worldliness, and the program of an answer is our main task.

I am not sure whether what I have to say in the following chapters is a prediction or a program. Perhaps it is simply a utopia. If there should be a catastrophe of our civilization which would strip the church of some of its cultural and organizational ballast, my hope is that the church which would emerge from the catastrophe might look something like the church I will describe in the coming chapters. Otherwise, the following is more a program, which I expect to be realizable only here and there by desperate efforts. But two or three together are always enough. As to completeness or precise formulation, I make no claim at all for what follows. But sometimes it is unwise to refine ideas to perfect precision. They may lose both their time and their hearers.

As soon as one penetrates Thomas Altizer's cloudy and sometimes frivolous terminology, one realizes that he has grasped with exceptional energy the problem of religious Christianity and the necessity and pain of overcoming it. I understand the nature of religion much as he does—this reflects, no doubt, our common dependence on Eliade and Kerenyi. It is, therefore, all the more distressing to have to judge his "gospel" as a triumph of religion.

Religion is the retreat from time and history to timelessness. The word which Christianity has to hearken to is, in direct challenge to religion's security in how it has always been, an incarnate word, a word which sounds in time and calls us to the events of time as our hope and task, and which therefore is an eschatological word, cutting us off from the past and giving us the future as our life. So far we agree.

But then Altizer decrees that we must sever this word, as we are now called to hear and speak it, from being in any way a word about the past Jesus. We must rather always receive this word *de novo* from the prophets of our own day, with no prejudgment of its content. It is indeed plain that how to talk of the past Jesus as the future who frees us from the past is indeed the difficult point in the project of an antireligious gospel, and is the point where the halfhearted have hedged and started to talk about "On the other hand . . ." But if we seek to evade this difficulty, then the word which calls us to the future has no descriptive content, and the future to which it calls is not a particular future event but abstract futurity, rather in the style of Bultmann's weaker thought. This futurity is but a new variety of timelessness; time is the expectation of concrete occurrences. Altizer's eschatological consummation differs, he says, from the religious penetration to the ground of being only in that religion finds that ground in the past and eschatological faith finds it in the future. But where future means futurity, this is not a difference. Primal time and final time are identical, are mere forms of eternity, both in mysticism and pure apocalypticism. Only the occurrence of God as a describable historical event breaks this pattern.

Thus Altizer constructs his gospel simply as the negative mirror-image of religion. Since the coincidence of opposites is, as he stresses, a basic principle of religion, this produces only an especially intense religiosity, as in Buddhism. Can this be because Altizer has no experience of the radical reformation gospel which killed our religion? And so has only that death itself from which to construct for himself some meaning?

II. THEOLOGY: JESUS VERSUS THE ETERNAL

The Death of God

Is it true that God is dead? Banally, that depends on what you mean. "God is dead" could mean that there never really was such a being, but that people thought there was, and that something has now happened to discover the truth to us. This would make sense—whether true or not. Or "God is dead" could mean that there used to be such a being but that something has happened so that now there is not. Whether such an assertion could make any sense at all depends on several things, especially and again banally on what or whom you mean by "God."

Those who lately have been using the slogan have evidently been trying to follow Nietzsche. What Nietzsche meant is fairly plain. He meant that there really had used to be a God and that the drive for truth which religion itself kindles had destroyed him. By "God" he meant the deity of standard Christian theology, the fusion of Platonism's changeless Good, Beauty, and Truth with the Father of Jesus Christ.

There are formidable difficulties in Nietzsche's assertion if it is taken woodenly. For the God of standard theology is, as an inheritance from the Platonist side, supposed to be omnipotent, omniscient, and eternal. It would seem to be nonsense to speak of the death of such a being: clearly, if there ever was an eternal being, then he is still around. The recent Christian Nietzscheans appear to be hung up on this difficulty and largely to have abandoned all attempt to make sense.

Nietzsche himself was in a less desperate case, since he was skeptical in general about the reality of things "out there" separate from our interpretation of the world. For him, all there was to God or to anything else was our habit of interpreting and dealing with the chaos of existence in a particular way. There are atoms because we find it convenient to posit such entities to make our calculations work out. There is a God if we need him, pray to him, live as if he existed. If that need vanishes, so does God, for that is all there was to him.

We need not share Nietzsche's general skepticism, but with respect to the God of religion, he is our prophet. The God who is the sum of all the gods and "values" and "higher ideals" of religion, the God who is the chief inhabitant and embodiment of religion's special world, existed only as the creation of our fears and dreams. He existed as the creation of our longing for an author to our tale in whose mind the conclusion of it could be already enacted. We have found this out, and that has killed him. The God of religion was real as a cultural force, as a word that lived in our tradition and dominated our ideas of good and bad, our political will, our art, our choices of all sorts. This cultural force has indeed died. Those who reject religion now usually do so not because they find it necessary to disbelieve in God, but simply because the whole matter seems insignificant. Indeed, there is the suspicion that many who say they are religious find this possible just because it makes so little difference anyway.

Now the question is, what does this mean for theology? What does it mean for our talking about God—which is what "theology" means? Are we to become atheists? Perhaps "Christian atheists" —whatever that might be? I wish to suggest the opposite possibility. Always before, the preachers of the gospel have had to assume that man already believed in God-in-general and have had to tell the gospel merely as additional information about him. We have had to say: "God—of whom you already believe that he is responsible for your existence, that he is omnipresent, etc.—has also done this, he has sent his Son to you." Now the death of the God of religion has freed us from this detour.

Instead of being only an added chapter to our theology, what the gospel says about the events around Jesus can now become the whole of it. We are free to develop a teaching about God which is in its entirety nothing but the explication of what happened with Jesus. Thereby also all our talk of what happened with Jesus will become talk about God—so that Christian theology will become what its name has always suggested, one great statement of God.

Whether we continue to use the *word* "God" will be a matter of strategy only. The need to which religion responded with its dreams of God is still there—it is identical with the act of living as a mortal man. There is a being of whom we wish to say that that need is need of him—the one who lived the life of Jesus of Nazareth. And we will have to have some way of speaking which will bring the two together.

So also we will continue to address our gospel, our talk about Jesus, to the theology our hearers already have, but we will no longer appeal to their belief in God but to their experience of no longer believing. We will no longer appeal to the illusions by which we have stilled our longings, but to the fact of the discovered or discoverable impossibility of stilling those longings. "God is dead" will not be our message or theology. It will, however, be the natural theology which we will expect to find in our hearers. For the gospel, this natural theology will be a far more appropriate "point of attachment" than we have ever had before.

That we do have a natural theology becomes plain if we ask: If the word "God" is dead, why can we not leave it alone? Why can we not desist from reiterating how meaningless this meaningless word is? Why will this empty sound not disappear? We remain hooked on the word "God" because by its very emptiness it serves to express a loss. It is imposed on us, almost as a fate, by the absence of something we cannot do without. "God" is the name for the darkness of that future which calls us, the name for what ought to be there to receive us.

"God is not." What does this meaninglessness do in our lives? It is our natural theology. It is a lament we cannot cease from. It is a fate imposed on us. Therefore to fully understand we must expand it: "God is not—but ought to be." "God is not—yet." This is the true content of our bereavement.

The one who is not yet, the future as post-religious man faces it in its blankness and terror—this absence is real enough. We name it "God." We too have our wholly negative natural theology. Perhaps some day it too will be gone and men will simply live in the present, content in the sciences and common sense. Then they will no longer be men. The Apocalypse tells us that God will intervene before then.

"Jesus is God." Clearly, if we are to say this, the word "God" must mean something prior to our application of it to Jesus. Theology indeed depends on natural theology. We, too, possess one. But with our word "God" we bring to Jesus no rich fund of prior knowledge, no fine list of attributes and honors, as did our fathers. We bring an absence and a lack, a denial and a judgment. We bring an empty place for hope.

This is quite a different natural theology than that which we used to carry when we named Jesus God, but surely it is no less adapted to our need to speak of Christ than the most glorious evocation of Goodness, Beauty, and Truth. For all our words, if he truly is, are absolutely inadequate. Indeed, it is possible that precisely in its negativity it is the most honest confession of what God wills us to know of himself prior to Christ: ". . . the *wrath* of God is revealed from heaven . . ."

Just because the word "God" is a mere lack on our lips, it provides the empty place for Christ to fill. Whenever the church has thought it knew all about God anyway and merely recognized him in Christ, it has been on the way to paganism. A truly Christian doctrine of God is a description of Jesus Christ. It says that this man shall come and every knee shall bow. It says that he is the one who has hidden behind the mask of the absent "God."

Faith's Use of "God"

In our religious use of "God" we cry out to the future in the hope of some answer that will assure us there is point to life. And in our religion we do indeed apprehend the future— but against our hope and intention it is the future's emptiness, its blankness and terror, that we apprehend. All our religious activity and speculation is but the attempt to evade this awful experience at its own heart. The religious question, asked honestly and to the end, carries its own annihilating answer: "What is the meaning of life?" "There is none." In our religiosity we apprehend only the empty place where the goal of life should be, the path of life that peters out in the desert before us. "God" evokes a loss, the word is wrung from us by the absence of what we cannot do without. It is the name of the one who ought to be waiting to receive us—but is not. "God" haunts us as the inescapable evocation of the emptiness of human existence.

A worldly culture is simply one in which the evasions of religion are stripped from the awful experience which they both evoke and try to hide—or at least become patently evasions. The experience is still there, and to it the gospel must now as always be addressed. This is why believers speak of "God."

Believers have used this fatal word "God" to say something we must say in talking rightly about Jesus of Nazareth. Otherwise we would have had every reason to eschew altogether talking about God, for we know the judgment and despair hidden in all talk of God, and that by indulging in it we entangle ourselves in the very religion we speak to overcome. We have called Jesus the "Son of God" or the "Revelation of God" or straight-out "God" in order to say of him: What happened in his life is what is going to happen at the end of our stories, i.e., on the day that for each of us can be dated by the event of death. If "God" means "the one who will settle our fate," then "Jesus is God" means "Jesus is the one who will settle our fate." When we hear his story, we are told of the conclusion of our lives, we are told that utter self-giving of one man for another is what will finish and conclude our struggle or lack of struggle. When I get hooked on Jesus' story, it is decided that "died for his enemies" will be the last line in my history.

When we have said "Jesus is God," we have been saying: Suddenly, now that he has happened, our lives have a goal. Suddenly the dark future, without ceasing to be dark, has become our future *for* which we can live. For the future is that this man Jesus, whose life is life for us and who calls us to live for him, is coming. We can now narrate the point of our lives, and the narration begins "and Jesus came preaching the kingdom of God . . ." We go to meet someone. Jesus was the future happening, the absolute darkness become our true goal.

The dark future does not thereby become less unpredictable, less new. For if what will end our lives is the meeting with a man, then it will be that kind of event which is the very occasion of all freedom, all creativity, all wonderful and unpredictable new starts. Nevertheless, if "Jesus" is the name of the mystery of the future, we can know that it is a mystery of life, not of death. Its unpredictability is the blessed unpredictability of human love when it succeeds, not the fearsome unpredictability of fate.

The meaning of human actions is always settled by what comes of them. What I truly am and what, if anything, the deeds of my life are worth will be settled only by the last judgment. If no judge comes and death is simply a cessation, that too will be a judgment: that my life meant nothing. The gospel says that Jesus will be the last judge. If this is so, then the future is truly open, then the content of the last judgment is truly unpredictable, for he will be a loving judge. The meanings he will find in the false starts, unfinished undertakings, and petty hatreds of our lives will be past all imagining, for *we* can find *no* meaning in them. His judgment will be unpredictable in the way forgiveness is, not in the way of a doubtful case before a scrupulous judge.

According to the gospel, our destiny is to become involved in the life of Jesus of Nazareth, to play roles in the story of his love for his fellow men. There will be a conclusion of our lives, marked as the conclusion by death—and he will be it. Death will be the occasion of Jesus addressing us in love and of our being at last utterly freed from ourselves so as to be able to respond to such an address. I do not mean this in any attenuated or spooky sense: I am talking about something that will happen between the man Jesus of Nazareth and other men—you and me. The end will be that, together with Jesus and because of what he will say to us, we will be able to interpret our lives and all that has happened in them as incidents in his life of love for his and our fellows. The end will be that he with us will work out the meaning of all we have done and all that has happened to us, as love. In his address and our response, we will perform our lives for him and each other as offerings of love. This performance will never end, for it will *be* the end.

In these last paragraphs, we have talked about Jesus of Nazareth in a certain way: as a particular man of past history, who is also our last future at the day timed by death. In so doing we have been talking about the reality for which believers use "God." The personal history enacted by this man, proclaimed as the event which brackets us in time—this is God. There is no way around the act of love which Jesus got done in life. If we ask what is responsible for our being here, it is that will which was this love. We were put here to provide objects of that love. If we ask what will come of us, it is that we will be completely involved with Jesus. To make this claim is to talk about God. What Christians mean by "God" is the way in which we both come from and go to what happened with Jesus of Nazareth.

God is what Jesus of Nazareth accomplished in life, what got done in the course of his history. God is the future, the hopes and possibilities, opened by the events of this man's life. "God is love" is something the church has always said, and meant by this more than that being loving was just one of God's characteristics. Therefore the temptation has always been there to turn the sentence around: "Love is God." Much of current popular theology succumbs to this temptation and thereby, far from overcoming religion, capitulates to it for good. There is no such thing as love-in-general—this is the prize example of religion's dream-reality. Nevertheless, if we remember the particularity of all real love, there is a closely related proposition we can and must use: "*Jesus'* love is God." The act of love that was enacted in this man's life brackets us in time. We are going to it—full involvement in it is what will conclude our lives. We also come from it—it is the reason we are here.

Is "God" then just another name for Jesus? Not quite. We may very well say: "God is Jesus." Yet in our worship and preaching such language has always been matched by language like "God *in* Christ," "Father *of* Christ," "Son *of* God." A direct identification of the man Jesus of Nazareth and God would make "a god" out of Jesus, which would bring us back to religion. God is the one "*in*" Christ, the father "*of*" Christ. What does this mean? God is the miracle that this man of our past is the coming future. God is the mystery of time, the mystery that we can live *for* someone, for Jesus. God is the miracle that we have this identifiable and knowable person as a destiny. God is what happens between Jesus and us. He is what happens when we hear Jesus' story as the news of our destiny, and he is what will happen on the day when a meeting with Jesus will fulfill our destiny.

"God is in Christ." What does this mean? Every person is who and what he is only from the future, only by the choosing and being chosen in which he lives for his particular hopes. The choice of love and self-sacrifice by which Jesus was who and what he will be, is one event with the choice by which God is who and what he is, by which God is God. That is, Jesus' choice to be the Crucified is also the choice by which he and we together are chosen to a final destiny of *being* loved. Therefore the story which Jesus wrote by the choices of his life, the story which begins "And Jesus came into Galilee, preaching . . . ," is the story about God. The history of Jesus' choosing, the history of which the "Apostles'" and "Nicene" creeds give summaries, is the history of God. If asked, "What is God like?" we answer as we always do about persons; we say, "Well, he is the one who . . ."—where what follows the "who" is narrative of what happened with Jesus.

We can say the same thing as in the last two paragraphs this way too: What any person is, is what he has to say. Better, what any person is, is what can be said on account of him. What any person is, is what "comes to word" through his life, what can be said because he lived. The question of a man's being is: Does the word "love" seem appropriate in conversation with and about him? Or the word "free"? Or "future"? We are, moreover, creators of language. Each of us adds to the language. As any personality speaks of "freedom" or of "destiny" or of "love," these words come to mean something slightly new and different than before. The great among us create new words and whole new languages. And where language is added to, there some reality comes to speech, there we can talk of something—we can know and relate to something—that we could not talk of before.

What comes to word in Jesus' life, what can be spoken of on account of him, is God—the God, that is, whom Christians worship. In the course of telling Jesus' story it is appropriate and possible to speak of God without falling into religion. Thus Jesus' being, what he has to say, is God. Moreover, this word in which God comes to speech has a definite descriptive content; it is a narrative about a historical person and what he is like. This description is, then, description also of God. "What is God like?" "He is like Jesus."

Both the question "Who is God?" and "What is God?" can therefore be given straightforward and unsupernatural answers by the believer, by the one who has become involved in the talk about Jesus. We turn now directly to these questions.

Who Is God?

To the question "Who is God?" the answer of believers has always been "He is the one who raised Jesus from the dead." This has not been intended as some additional information about a God otherwise identified. "The one who raised Jesus from the dead" is the believer's identification of God, his answer to the question of who it is that he worships instead of the God of religion. "Whoever raised Jesus, he is God." The claim and hope of faith is that the one who raised Jesus from the dead will at the end of the human story show that he is the one who will decide all human destiny, that he is "God."

There is another expression which has been a standard name of the Christian God: "The Triune God." Asked, "Which god do you worship?" the church has replied, "We worship the triune one." The first point to get across is that to the question "Who is God?", "The Triune God" and "The one who raised Jesus" are the same answer. If God raised Jesus, then God is separate from Jesus. Yet apart from what happens with Jesus, there is no God; God's reality *is* the history of Jesus. "God is triune" is merely

the attempt to say both of these in one slogan. The doctrine of
the Trinity is commonly regarded as the most abstruse part
of traditional Christian doctrine—especially by those who have
no idea what it says. It appears abstruse only because it rep-
resents the anti-supernaturalist thrust of the Christian message
in a context of generally religious identifications of God. "God
is the Triune God" is but a more analytical way of saying that
he is the one who raised Jesus from the dead.

The doctrine of the Trinity states the shape in time of the
event we live from. It is what happened with Jesus of Nazareth
that is this event. At the center, therefore, there is the particular
individual historical man Jesus. What he does refers both forward
and backward in time. The word which came to utterance with
him, the gospel, calls us to reappropriate our beginning. We are
called to reconsider the mystery of our being here, of the in-
explicable givenness of life and a world: "Why is there anything
at all? Why not rather nothing?" Most particularly, "Why am I?"
Now, once the gospel has intruded, we have to take up this
question in the course of our talk about Jesus Christ. We now
have him as the one who puts the question to us. We also
have "So that he might love you" as a proposed answer. As to
the future, it is precisely our future that the gospel claims Jesus
is. His whole life as narrated by the gospel is a summons to
consider what will come of us and a claim that meeting with
him is what will come of us.

Thus the shape of what happened and will happen with Jesus
is this: Origin and Fulfillment crossing in the History between
Jesus and us. God is God Creator, God Perfector, and God
Revealer; he is God past, God future, and God present; he is
God the Father, God the Spirit, and God the Son. If you will,
Creation, Fulfillment, and Revelation are the plot of God's life,
the plot of his life-for-us in what happens with Jesus Christ.

All that is now necessary is the antireligious denial that there is
any "essence" or "deeper reality" or "ultimate mystery" of God
"behind" or "above" or "within" these three events of God's
life for us, of what happened with Jesus, to have the full
classical doctrine of the Trinity. God is the event of Jesus' love

as an event in history; and he is the event of that love as what put me here; and he is the event of that love as what will accomplish the purpose of my being here. He is these three events and that is all that he is.

"Who is God?" He is the one whose life is these three events. What happens with Jesus in and to this world of time is not the manifestation or working-out or mirroring of some superior reality above time. God was our past, he will be our future, and he is both now in what happens historically between Jesus and us. This enclosure of our lives in time is not to be explained in terms of a deeper, timeless reality of God above his temporal reality. In God, past, future, and present are both one event and three— "one God in three persons"—and this is not to be explained by putting the "real" God in a dream-realm beyond time. It is rather simply the ultimate fact *about* time: God is the occurrence *now* of a *past* event as our *future*, he is Jesus' love as origin and goal—and it is only this occurrence which gives us time at all; only over against this occurrence are we those who live in the present for future hopes and plans and as we do so carry with us our pasts as materials and impediments.

Every person is what he is in that he chooses and fails to choose to be it. I, for example, am the would-be author of this book in the act of positing myself as the author, in the choice and decision in which I become the author. God is the one God in three acts of choice. He seizes his one being and lives and is his one concrete story and personality in three simultaneous deeds of choice. He is God the loving lord in the way of creating. He is God the loving lord in the way of fulfilling. He is God the loving lord in the way of revealing. And there is no timeless being above this story in whom these three choices hang together. They hang together as choices, as life, indeed as the human life of Jesus.

All this seems very abstract. Yet it is but the attempt to talk about a God who is everything but abstract. Luther said it better: "Let us know no other God than the babe in the lap and at the breasts of his mother." Where are we to seek God? We are to seek him not at all. For he is not off anywhere. He is not in some religious special realm. As you read these words about Jesus, something is happening between you and me and this babe, if only that your conviction is being strengthened that it is all nonsense. It is the claim of what is said here that this event that is now happening in your life has happened also as the origin of your life and will happen to fulfill it. This event is what we worship.

Let us go one more step to the final audacity of the doctrine of the Trinity, using the traditional language. The traditional doctrine asserts that the persons of the Trinity are identical with their relations to each other. It is not that there is first the Father who then also begets the Son: begetting the Son is all there is to being the Father. It is only by their relations to each other that the persons subsist as persons. Does this kind of talk say anything at all? I think it does. Each person of the Trinity *is* life for the others with nothing held back. Since there is no essence of God behind the persons, God, therefore, is the sacrificial life of persons for each other.

Nor is God the mutual self-giving either of supernatural persons in eternity or of all persons in general, for the "second person" is the particular man Jesus of Nazareth. God is that particular interpersonal life which takes place where Jesus of Nazareth lives and acts in self-forgetfulness. It is popular now to say that something or other called the "depth" of interpersonal relations is, in general, God. This is too religious. It is the particular self-sacrificing interpersonal relations which Jesus of Nazareth had and will have which are God, and not in mysterious depths but just as the social, ethical, etc., relations that they were and will be. As we become involved with him through the story about him—in the same way, then, as we become involved with any figure of history—we play roles in the life-story of God. Yet we are not God, as simply as Jesus of Nazareth was and will be one person and I another, as simply as, if indeed he comes to decide our destiny, then he will do it and not we.

An antireligious identification of God will be one where the doctrine of the Trinity emerges from being one item in our doctrine of God to become the whole of it, to become our only identification of God. We said earlier that believers speak of God only in phrases like "the God of Jesus Christ," "the Father of Christ," "the God who raised Jesus," and the like. We do not name God apart from naming the historical figure Jesus—this would be supernaturalism. Neither do we identify God and Jesus —this would be a very primitive religiosity indeed. We say always "the God *of* Christ." Only in speaking so of God can we use "God" against religion. The doctrine of the Trinity as here sketched is the attempt at a specification of the God who must be spoken of in this way. It is the only possible antireligious doctrine of God.

What Is God?

What then is God? If he is this God?

God is real for us as history; we have to do with him when we have to do with a certain event through the story about it. God has not been with us through formulae or oracles or visions but through a life-history. Unless we are to make the religious leap to a God behind what happens with and to us in this history, this means that God himself is an event, a deed, an act. For God, to be is to do, to become.

God's choosing and acting is not transcended by some static core of his being. With us, it always seems to make sense to say that when I do something, there is a something-or-other named by the "I" which remains aloof and unchanged by what I do. Not so with God. He is not a such-and-such who then, as such-and-such, does so-and-so. God is what he does. Indeed, he is the doing of it. He *is* love.

We may put it this way: God does not exist, like a stone or an atom or even like a man. God happens.

God is an event. Which? The identity of God is that he is the Trinity. Therefore the event that God is, is exactly the event of that work in which he lives as our God, the event of his turning to us, of his judging and accepting us. God lives his life in creating, revealing, and fulfilling. God happens—and the happening that he is, is that which happens to us with Jesus Christ.

We must next say that the event which is God is a free event. If God is triune, then he needs no other persons to live in interpersonal action and life. If God is triune, he is in himself a "we," a fellowship, a situation of challenge and response and activity. He is "I" and "you," and so "we"; he is the one person, God, as a "we." All persons are what they are only by the fellowship in which they live. God is in himself fellowship, and in and through that fellowship is one personal being. Since God is fellowship for himself, he is who and what he is entirely of himself, entirely autonomously. That is, God is who and what he is freely. This freedom is not the abstract freedom of an isolated subject who can in his isolation do what he chooses. It is the authentic freedom which arises as the challenges and possibilities which persons pose to each other.

God is free. He himself decides who and what he shall be. That he is God and what sort of God he is, is his own choice. We can assign no reasons why there is a God nor why he is as he is. Nor can God, except as he in fact chooses to live for particular purposes. The existence and nature of God are purely contingent. Jesus might not have chosen as he did, might not have been the particular person he in fact was, and therefore there might have been no God or there might have been some other God—except that God has in fact chosen to be God and to be the God that he is. God is purely contingent. Just so he is "absolute."

If, therefore, we ask what sort of event God is, the answer is: God is a decision. God is his own decision. What happens that is the happening of God? A decision is made. We press the "what" one more step and ask: The making of what decision is God happening? We answer: Jesus' decision about us. In every life, something is decided. What Jesus decided in his life was to be *for* us no matter what. The gospel says that this decision of Jesus is the final one about us, the last judgment which settles our destiny. That is, Jesus' decision not to resist evil is God.

The decision which is God is the decision which was made in Jesus' life to be with and for sinful men. God chooses us to be his, despite our rebellion. He chooses himself to be ours, despite our rejection. Indeed, he chooses to be ours precisely as the rejected one. He chose to happen for us as the Crucifixion, as the very event of our hatred and suffering—and is therefore the God who cannot be separated from us, for the very occurrence of what could have separated him from us he chose as his life.

Thus God's decision to love us, to bring our lives to fulfillment in mutual self-giving, cannot be altered by anything we do. Nor is it in any question from the side of God, for there is nothing to God beyond or above or behind this decision. God would not have had to be God for us; he chose to be. But he does so choose, and this decision *is* God.

We may as well let the awful word appear: we have been speaking for some time of "predestination." God is the decree that settles our destiny. Thus the doctrine of predestination is part of the doctrine of God; it is the attempt to say what sort of being God is. A God who was not the God of predestination would simply not be God, or at least not the God of the gospel.

The horrid reputation of the word "predestination" comes from two sources. The one is the objection which religion and religious people always make to truly believing ideas: "But do you mean to say that my deciding and willing and doing are not the last word?" The other is that this Christian doctrine of God does indeed, like the doctrine of the Trinity, present a demonic appearance in the context of religion.

We need not, however, fear the notion of predestination, once the God of predestination is distinguished from the God of religion. For where God is not a distant being beyond time, but what happens with Jesus of Nazareth, then the decree of predestination is not the arbitrary fiat of a tyrant, but rather the decision which is made about us as we hear Jesus' story and the claim this story makes. The decree of predestination is the decree of any man who says to me, "You are God's child, for Jesus' sake." The doctrine of predestination says that his saying this is the very reality of God, so that I can trust that what is said will be done in spite of everything.

This brings us to the final thing to be said of God, which sums up all the rest: God is a word. He is an address, a summons, a promise.

We live our lives in a sea of words. From all sides we are

challenged, informed, corrected, obligated, comforted. This is what makes us men, for human life is life for the future, and the possibility of this is given by language. I can live for what I am not yet only in that I am confronted by someone other than, different from, me, who offers me possibilities strange to what I already am; that is, I can live for what I am not yet only in that I live in communication.

The first question about any utterance is, therefore, what future does it open up? What can be different because this word has been spoken? "I do" opens up the future of two people as a future with each other; a scientific hypothesis opens a particular set of experiments to be carried out. If the future opened by the speaking of a word is my last future, if it can be dated by death, then the speaking of this word is the reality for us of God.

The gospel is such a word. We said earlier that God was the mystery of time by which we have the historical person Jesus as the one we go to meet, by which he brackets us in time. Now we can say, God is the *saying* of the gospel, the proclaiming to me of the story of Jesus as the tale of my destiny. Future and past come together, not in some changeless thing, but in the event of the address of the gospel, in one man's speaking to another the story and claim of Jesus. This event is God.

Is God, then, a mere category or event of our existence? Not at all. The speaking which God is has straightforward descriptive content. It is narrative about a figure of history, Jesus of Nazareth, and makes concrete predictions about someone who will come at the end of our ways, and what will happen then. Neither the Jesus of history nor the coming Lord is created by us in any way. The word in which God occurs is a word about them.

Moreover, it is not that we proclaim Jesus to each other that makes him the one in whom God happens. On the contrary, our proclaiming is the event of God only because it is about Jesus. What the proclamation says is exactly "He *was* God loving you," prior to our proclaiming.

How can this be? Only if the event of Jesus was a proclaimed event before it was ever proclaimed by or to us. Here again we arrive at the doctrine of the Trinity, of a God who in himself is Speaker and Hearer. God is the saying of the story about Jesus, and is this independently of having us for speakers or hearers.

God is, therefore, a conversation. All true words are conversational, they are spoken by one person to another. The conversation which God is, is the word of love spoken to us. But God is free; he does not need us to be what he is, to be a true, conversational, word. God is not merely part with us of the conversation about our destiny. He could have been a conversation which excluded us. For he is in himself Speaker, Word, and Accomplished Communication; he is in himself address and response. He is triune.

The "could" in the paragraph above marks the freedom of the word which is God. It marks God as the Creator, who would have happened even if his creatures had not. It marks also the awful possibility of God speaking about us but not to us, the possibility of damnation. But in the word which God does in fact speak to us, the freedom of the conversation which is God is that the course of the conversation is not bound by our response, that to our "I hate" we receive as response "You are loved." As the triune word, God is the word of forgiveness.

Again the God of Religion

Not only Christians live between past and future. Not only, therefore, when the gospel is spoken is God spoken. Whenever a man is called out of what he already is toward a future which opens before him as something new and unpredictable, God is speaking. A foreman shouting, "What the hell you doing? You want to get fired?" can be a word of God. Nor do we need to know that a word is God's for it to be his. What counts is not how we feel about a word but what it in fact does to us.

Religion has been our standard way of replying to the address of God. Religion, we have said, is our attempt to create for ourselves a secure final future. Although the attempt cannot succeed, so that religion creates illusions, what makes us seek the future is no illusion. We are driven to the future by the voices of life itself, by the voices which without cease summon us, obligate us, demand of us, promise us: the voices of our families, of the organs of society, of the codes of our professions and the internal necessities of our labors, and then perhaps of the panhandler who asks for a half-dollar. What makes us seek the future is no illusion—and it is God.

The God of religion was an illusion. We invented him. When, however, we have hearkened to and served him, we have been responding to the very real word of the true God, the word which *is* God. If now life's demand that we move on to death no longer has the comforting accent of the God of religion, the demand itself rings all the clearer.

The God of the gospel is, therefore, no stranger. We always have already known him, whether as the God of religion or as the speaking absence of the God of religion. The conversation with God in which we hear the gospel story and try to respond in prayer and praise is one we have always already been involved in. It is simply the conversation which is life itself, our ordinary secular life of address and response. The question is: What is said in this conversation? The voice of religion or of the loss of religion, the voice we have always already heard, tells a tale of death. The story of Jesus is a story of death and resurrection. The God of religion and the God of the gospel are, after all, the same. The one is the God of death and the other the God of life—and they are one as two steps in one history, the history of Jesus' death and resurrection and of ours.

This chapter is an attempt to carry out Bonhoeffer's program. Thus it is an attempt to do what William Hamilton says may someday be done but not now.

According to Hamilton, the religious a priori is gone, in that nowhere in human experience do we now *need* God. We can make it, intellectually and morally, without him. So the previous basis of our worship and faith is gone, and religion, as the "system . . . in which God . . . serves as fulfiller of needs or solver of problems" is a lost possibility.

Yet Hamilton is not an ordinary atheist. He waits, he says, for God to return. This waiting means: (1) waiting for the possibility of a way of talking about God which will not be needing him but rather enjoying him exactly as the one we do not need, and (2) assuming the place in the world of those bereft of religious security and just so being in Jesus' place.

What we all feel could not be more lucidly said. Only one thing puzzles me: What would have to happen to make the new language possible? What precisely is Hamilton waiting for? Indeed, why must we wait at all to seek a new way of talking about God? Why not get on with the attempt? It sometimes seems that Hamilton is waiting for Jesus to be born, or perhaps for the Reformation. Both the miracle of God and the freed insight of man which make possible an antireligious doctrine of God have already happened. This does not guarantee that my attempt, or any other, will succeed. For the truth of our attempt to talk about God without using him, we must indeed wait. But this has been so since the first birth of faith.

III. WORSHIP: LITURGY DEMYTHOLOGIZED

Gatherings of believers for what is called worship are the heart of the life of the church. The present hollowness of our religious Christianity is both most apparent and most destructive of faith in this, that on the great majority of such occasions nothing whatever happens. We gather, we say prayers, we sing songs, we hear a discourse and some readings—and we leave with the distinct consciousness that we have accomplished nothing at all, that no event unique to this gathering has occurred. Much of what is meant by saying that religion is dead is that nothing happens in our worship, that precisely those most dedicated to Christ and their brothers are increasingly perceiving this, and that they are therefore seeking places "outside the church" where they can at least do something for their brothers.

What Is Worship?

When the church worships, what is it trying to do? The business of the church is telling and hearing the story of Jesus, as the story of the destiny of those who tell and hear; that is, the business of the church is telling and hearing the "gospel." Worship is the gathering of persons for this purpose. It is a gathering because telling and hearing are doings that take place only in groups, because language is communion. Two at least are needed.

Telling the gospel is a verbal performance, a talking. But it involves nonverbal performances also. Telling any genuine—i.e., interesting—story always is a dramatic enactment complete with nonverbal as well as verbal action, as anyone knows who has ever told a story into a microphone and found himself gesticulating to his unseeing audience. In the particular case of the gospel story this is redoubled. For this narrative is made with the claim that nothing less than the destiny of the hearers is being narrated. The one who hears this story hears his own last judgment. To tell this story to someone is, therefore, to commit an act of violence upon him, it is to *do* something decisive to him. It is to utter "performatively," to use words in such a way as not merely to describe a reality, but to create it. So when the dignitary says, "I christen thee U. S. S. *Himalaya*," the ship thereby acquires this name. Before the act of utterance, the ship had no name; now it has exactly this one, and the new situation was created by the act of speaking. When the priest says, "I declare unto you the forgiveness of all your sins," or, "Jesus is your lord," he speaks in this same way.

The act of telling this story is itself, therefore, a performance, a doing of the story rather than a mere telling about it. It is an enactment. The acting-out which thus accompanies the verbal telling of the gospel we call sacraments, culminating in the Eucharist, where we quite literally take the roles of Jesus and the apostles and act out a decisive segment of the gospel story upon each other.

Hearing too is an action. The genuine hearer labors, both on his understanding of the matter and on his relation to the speaker. And this labor is by no means a purely invisible, "mental" labor. It includes sitting, standing, squinting, writing, etc. Beyond this, if what is being said is performed in order to be said, then hearing too means taking a role in the performance. Hence bowing, kneeling, gesturing, and—at the high point—literal play-acting are essential also to the hearing side of Christian worship.

Thus Christian worship is a gathering around a story in which what is told about also occurs as an enactment in the lives of the tellers and hearers: they *do* this enactment and this doing is as much an event in their lives as any other and remains as a part of their histories. Radically put, worship is an event which is the occurring in our lives of what happened with Jesus. Worship is the occurrence of our involvement now with the past Jesus.

Supernaturalist Worship

The problem is that the bridge in worship between what happened with Jesus and the present content of our lives has been traditionally provided by one or more supernatural beings, supposed present in the action of worship as actors and/or objects of action. Most important, Christian worshipers have regarded Jesus Christ in this way. The presumed presence in the act of worship of an invisible and sacred being, identified with the Jesus of the New Testament witness, has functioned as the bridge between what happened with the past Jesus and the worshipers' present existence. It has done so in the following way: Jesus is supposed to be present as a thing in addition to the worshipers, furniture, etc. His presence is analogous to their presence, though invisible, inaudible, and intangible. The Jesus who is so present is the reigning inhabitant of heaven and so in charge of the final destiny of the worshipers. What he does as present is therefore a decisive occurrence in their lives. So the one end of the bridge is secured. The destiny which Jesus in fact has to give is then supposed to be in some way the result of what he did and suffered in his past life on earth, and is also in some way a repetition or reflection of that life. Thus Jesus' presence as a supernatural being is the bridge between his past doing and suffering and the present event in the worshipers' lives.

Protestants and Catholics have typically dealt with this extra being, "Jesus," in different ways. Protestants evoke him by talking about him. "Confess your sins to Jesus, and he will forgive," we say. "Jesus is always with you, as you do your work, or as you . . ." The most jarring are usages like, "Can you take Jesus with you into a tavern?" or from those of opposite culture, "Will you follow Jesus into the secular world?" The pattern is that Jesus is bespoken in the third person—and then subsequently, of course, in the second person—as an additional present something who can, as such a thing, be described and who is by virtue of the character and capabilities ascribed to him in this description at once the continuation of the known past Jesus of Nazareth and the giver of the destiny of the worshipers.

Catholics have more typically located the supernatural Jesus as the imperceptible substance on the altar, hidden behind the perceptible characteristics of bread and wine. Since this supernatural Jesus is himself invisible and hidden behind what appears on the altar, words are also in this case required to locate him. But the words used in Catholic worship tend all to center around description of the supernatural being in the sacramental elements—insofar, that is, as they are not of the same sort as just described for Protestantism.

The problem is that we no longer apprehend supernatural beings, and so not the supernatural Jesus of traditional worship. When we are told, for example, to "accept Jesus," we do not know what exactly we are to do. The man sitting next to me I can accept: I can shake his hand, invite him to dinner, listen to his tale of woe. But how do this sort of thing with Jesus? The nearest we come to a vision of a supernaturally present Jesus is the notion of a sort of poltergeist who lives in church but is also to accompany us—rather over the left shoulder —in our "daily life."

Insofar as the supernatural Jesus is no longer experienced as a present entity in worship, the two poles of Christian worship —the past events narrated by the gospel and the occurring history of the worshipers—tend to disconnect. When this happens, the act of worship is replaced by other acts, even though many of the words and gestures which formerly belonged to the act of worship continue to be reiterated. This happens slightly differently in Protestant and Catholic traditions.

When Protestantism's talking fails to evoke the supernatural Jesus, and the two poles of Christian worship thus fall apart, what is left is talk *about* the past Jesus of Nazareth on the one hand and one or another sort of existential address to the worshipers on the other. What now occurs at the time and place previously given to worship may be a moral address, a sociology seminar, a songfest, a political meeting, a group therapy session, or perhaps even a lecture on dogmatics—provided, of course, with suitable opening and closing exercises called, for old times' sake, "the liturgy."

There is no future whatever in our secular culture for Protestant worship as hitherto conducted. It cannot last another twenty years. This is scarcely a prophecy; in many Protestant "churches" it is already a generation since any worshiping has been done. Meetings will no doubt continue to flourish in the buildings called "churches" so long as people need moral address, sociological discussion, etc., but nothing which it would be useful to call "worship" will occur.

If Protestant worship disintegrates to moralism, Catholic worship turns to superstition. When one is unable to apprehend a supernatural "substance" where he sees and feels bread and wine, one has two possibilities: one may come to apprehend the sacramental elements as "symbols" of "spiritual truths," as, in effect, words. On this path one will end in Protestantism and the previously described difficulties. Or one may be led, whatever his theories, in practice to simply worship the bread, wine, etc. I suspect that the actual piety of most Catholics is an unreconciled oscillation between these possibilities.

There is more staying power in superstition than in moralism, and more kinship to genuine worship. Thus there is now more actual life in the piety of Catholics than in that of Protestants. The triumph of the liturgical movement at Vatican II is providing less degenerate vehicles for that life—indeed, the best and most evangelical in use by any confession. This may well lead to a brief renewal of authentic Catholic worship, but far more radical changes than any mere reforms will be necessary if this renewal is not to be ephemeral in a secular society

I have contrasted Protestant and Catholic worship. This was done to show certain patterns, but the actual life of most congregations, of whatever confessions, is neither of these pure types. The most accurate description of the worship of most congregations is merely that it is utterly and suffocatingly trivial, for both reasons discussed above, and other besides. And little practical alleviation can be expected from current liturgical or theological reforms, though one should surely support them.

Two Requirements

Where do we go from here? Some say we should abandon worship, in the sense defined here, and seek our authenticity in the secular pursuits of life. Perhaps we should, but it seems clear that this would amount to abandoning Christian faith. Christianity without worship would be exactly Christianity without God—and the final triumph of religion.

If we are to continue worshiping, the situation is that we can no longer depend on an extra supernatural being, in addition to the worshipers and the objects they use, to unite what happened with Jesus and what happens to us now. The question here is not *whether* Christ is present in our worship; if we are to worship him, we must believe him present. The concern is to understand that presence, to indicate where to look for it as we worship. And the fundamental pointer is this: If it is not a ghostly extra entity that unites Jesus' past and our present and so is his presence to us, then it must be that this union occurs as the action of worship itself. What *we do* and suffer together around Jesus' story is itself his presence and posits the determination of our destinies by his. If this is to become clear, two requirements can be laid down for our worshiping.

Enactment

First, worship's character as an enactment must be made dominant and unmistakable. Our meetings must become in their entirety the acting-out of Jesus' story and destiny. An act of worship must be entirely a dramatic performance, in which all present play roles: a play about Jesus of Nazareth, with parts for his followers.

The place to begin will be the Eucharist. In Catholic worship, the character of the Eucharist as an enactment of Jesus' destiny is often clear. But any notion that the worshipers view a performance done by someone else must be abolished, not only in theory but by so ordering the action of worship that the idea becomes impossible. The Protestant spiritual-filling-station or "beautiful-ceremony" notions of the Eucharist are, of course, beneath discussion, as is that prime nonesuch, the private mass, and must also be made impossible by what is actually done in the celebration. All participants must have actions to perform which stretch over the entire celebration and are dramatically meaningful to the enactment of "the night in which he was betrayed."

The actual eating and drinking must be shaped to be exactly that. Perhaps the best ordinary arrangement would be for the congregation at a certain point in the action to seat itself at tables throughout the available space—rather as at a Boston Pops concert—and be served by deacons. The wine should be passed from hand to hand in loving cups. Catholic reservation for the priest and Protestant shot-glasses and/or grape juice are equally intolerable, or tolerable only on the crassly supernaturalist assumption that what is done is not important so long as some of the supernatural stuff gets in me or the wanted holy feelings are evoked. The bread should be a loaf demonstratively broken. From this central, rather realistically done acting-out, the dramatic involvement of the worshipers can spread to other, more expressionistic forms in the parts of the liturgy other than the actual communion.

Many such resources are already in the tradition: movement of the worshipers from one to another spatial relation to each other and to the dramatically significant objects, in procession or otherwise; such gestures as are clearly dramatically significant, either psychologically within the culture, such as kneeling, standing, bowing, or by some reference to the narrative content of the gospel story, as has the sign of the cross; the contrast of actions performed in light to others performed in shadow, and transfer from one to the other whether by movement of torches or by procession of the people; singing instead of saying; antiphony; etc. These actions may be referred more specifically yet to the narrative content of the gospel which is being enacted by being accompanied by and integrated into the actions of bands of dancers, mimes, or actors, who would function here somewhat analogously to the singing choir.

At the great festivals, which should by all means be retained or restored, the Eucharist and a pageant-like performance of the remembered event might coalesce entirely. A Christmas night Eucharist might have as its first part a pageant of the angels and shepherds, with the people as the shepherds, and as its mass of the faithful a celebration gathered, at the end of a procession, around a crib, with the bread and wine consecrated in the crib and thence distributed to those gathered around.

Modest beginnings are being made in some places. One congregation (Good Shepherd Congregation in Decorah, Iowa; R. David Berg, pastor) recently celebrated Palm Sunday with a procession of children to the church with a donkey carrying bread, wine, and a Bible. The congregation met the procession and all entered the nave together. The enactment of the entry of Jesus carried through the service.

One particular use of the procession and miming was with the reading of the lessons. The Old Testament lesson was from Zechariah, and deals with the coming of the king "on an ass, on a colt the foal of an ass" to destroy "the chariot," "the war horse," and "the battle bow." This was spoken by a choir; meanwhile two groups of small boys in front performed a simple dance representing war, countermarching through and recoiling from each other in columns, while the girls of their age froze in the center aisle in poses of fear. At the end of the lesson, the announcement "Lo, your King comes to you . . ." was repeated and thereupon a procession formed at the rear of the church and went down the center aisle: two acolytes with torches leading an acolyte carrying the Bible. When the procession reached the small girls, they broke their poses and threw palm branches before it; when it reached the warring boys it parted them and froze the dancers in position.

Standing between the parted warring groups, the acolyte with the Bible held it for the celebrant to read the gospel, the story of the entry into Jerusalem. Then the epistle lesson, the exhortation from the second chapter of Philippians to a mind of peace, was spoken; when the reading came at the end to "every knee shall bow," the previously warring boys knelt.

A second particular enactment used possibilities of the liturgy of the Eucharistic act itself. Children brought the loaves of bread and the wine—a bottle of Chianti—forward from the table to the altar. Then, just before the consecration, two acolytes received the filled chalice and a paten with bread from the celebrant and carried them throughout the church. As they marched back up to the altar to return the elements to the celebrant, the very smallest children ran before them scattering their palm branches.

It is plain that such acting-out of particular parts of the traditional liturgy still leaves us a great way from the ideal of this chapter. Moreover, the involvement of the rest of the congregation was in this case minimal. Much more should have been done to provide them with simple actions that would have been part of the enactment. Yet even these beginnings gave the Palm Sunday celebration a reality it had seldom possessed. As one worshiper said, "When we saw the beast coming across the fields we realized it could have really happened."

If a Eucharist which had become entirely enactment were to become the center of the congregation's life, other lesser dramas would gather around it. "How many sacraments" there are is entirely unimportant. Perhaps we can end this tiresome dispute by agreeing that all the life of the congregation should be enactment now of Jesus' destiny then, and that the Eucharist and baptism are the center. When we come to the simple devotions with which the church will surely never dispense, perhaps nothing more drastic will occur than that storytelling from Scripture is kept at the center.

It must not be thought that a sort of free-form worship extemporized from Sunday to Sunday is proposed. It is rather assumed that we begin at our proper place in the traditions of the Western mass, the Western service of baptism, and the hour-services. Moreover, the development of more explicitly dramatic forms of the services should not take place as a series of unrelated *ad hoc* experiments, but itself as a tradition, where elements tried and tested are retained and built upon. At the same time there should be wide freedom for creativity—as there was in the centuries when the liturgies were alive whose corpses are now guarded by the traditionalists.

For those denominations that still retain some connection to the central Western liturgical tradition, the step here proposed will, therefore, involve at the same time enlivening that connection. It will mean ceasing to do the given liturgy simply because it is given and seeking instead to do it as a vehicle of the living gospel. For those denominations which have broken with the tradition, it will mean recovering the connection. Which group has the harder wrench ahead is hard to say. Neither, at any rate, now has anything to lose worth keeping

The Unmythic Word

This acting-out is the acting which accompanies the telling of the gospel. What must this telling be like in a secular culture? The direct treatment of this question is dogmatics, the task of the previous chapter. Within our present topic, we bypass the dogmatic question, for which the acting-out is there for the sake of the word, and inquire what functions the word has for the enacting, and what the word must be like to fulfill them in a secular culture.

In the first place, words will occur as part of the dramatic acting-out itself, as dialogue. Here will occur—besides dramatic dialogue between participants—prayers, salutations, hymns, benedictions, and the like. In a secular culture, these latter must always be strictly appropriate to the dramatic action of which they are part. They must not, as it were, strike off on their own— to become independent talk with supernatural beings.

In the second place, the actions which the worshipers are performing must be identified by them as enactment of the story of Jesus of Nazareth, not someone else. This cannot be done by dramatic action itself, which is in itself always more or less historically ambiguous. Straightforward historical narration must therefore occur. Perhaps, as with the "words of institution," this will be done continuously with dialogue (worship is a rather Brechtian sort of drama anyway); perhaps separately, and then no doubt together with the third function of words in secularized worship, to the explanation of which we next turn. In a secular culture, this narration must be subject to critique by the results of historical-critical biblical research. If definitely legendary accounts are included, they must be treated as such.

We turn to the third function. The worshiping enactment is to be the occurrence of what happened with Jesus as an event in the life of the worshipers. It is plain, therefore, that as we have so far described it, something is missing. For when we act out a past event, the acting-out is indeed an occurrence in our lives, but not necessarily the past event itself that is acted out. When we act out the story of Washington, we ourselves do the acting, but we do not ourselves experience the crossing of the Delaware. The acted-out past event itself stays in the past. So the acting-out of, say, the gospel for a festival Sunday would be by itself a mere "dramatization" to "enrich" the day's program, and the very opposite of what we seek.

But the word, the word of proclamation, can free the acted-out event from the past into the future and present. Only the word can do this, for only in words of promise can the past be future. The word of proclamation narrates what happened with Jesus and asserts that what happened with Jesus will happen to you as your death-certain destiny, that the achievement of love-out-of-death which he enacted will fulfill your lives also. The word of proclamation is the assertion that you go to meet him, and will therefore conclude your lives by total involvement in his. It is the assertion that you have a destiny and that he is it, that his story tells of it.

In the word of proclamation, the story of the past Jesus is addressed to me as my future, as my possibility. If then it occurs that as an event in my life I enact this story as and when it is so proclaimed, then what happened with Jesus is not only the past which my action recalls, it is also the future in which my action will eventuate. Then this enacting is the event of my being destined to this destiny. In the context of this proclamation and not otherwise, our speaking and acting-out of the gospel story is, precisely as an enacting which is an occurrence in our lives like any other, our choosing and being chosen to this destiny which is real to us as the story of Jesus. It is, therefore, the event of our having Jesus' story as our story.

In the context of this proclamation, worship is the effective hearing of the proclamation, by which I am given love-out-of-death as my chosen future. As such it is the being done to me of what Jesus suffered himself and did to his followers. It is when

Jesus' story is enacted as not only past but also future that the enactment and not merely the enacting is a present event in our lives—and it is in the word of proclamation that the past can be future.

Thus it is by a word, by the address to me of Jesus' story as a promise and possibility of my story, that the event of worship can be and is the happening to us of what happened with Jesus. This brings us to a problem, and to the second requirement for worship in a secular society. For that style of the word we call myth has throughout human history had just this function of uniting past and present in worship—and myth is the very language of supernaturalism. Beings who embrace past and future in a changeless substantial presence which can be described and experienced, and so hold our fate in their hands, are the personages of all myths.

Our second requirement is: Myth cannot be the word of Christian worship in a secular culture. First, because a secular culture can be defined as one in which mythic assertions are bound to seem either false or pointless. Second, because myth is an essentially inappropriate word for Christian worship anyway, even though in traditional cultures it was unavoidable. Myth is the story of how things are always because they were so at the beginning. Myth tells the once-upon-a-time of eternity. It is therefore the indispensable language of religion. Myth mediates the future to the present by abolishing the futurity of the future, by creating an eternal now in which past, present, and future are all one. It is in this way that myth functions as the word by which what happened with the deity in primeval time happens now in worship. The security given by myth is the security of how it was, and therefore always will be. Myth is the word that overcomes change. Myth is exactly what the gospel contradicts.

Perhaps it was once necessary that the word of Christian worship was mythic in its form. But in a secular culture it is neither necessary nor possible. Yet what would it be for the word of worship not to be myth?

It would be to narrate the past story of Jesus and to proclaim this as the future without any attempt to mediate the presence of the past and future Jesus by *what* is said; rather, only by the present *saying* of it. The pattern of language which is to be avoided is of the sort: "Just as Jesus came to his disciples of old and as he will come at the end of days, so now he comes into our hearts," or ". . . onto the altar." Or again, "Jesus who forgave the dying thief and who one day will judge us all, will forgive you too if you will only come to him in prayer," or ". . . in confession." We must learn to leave off the last member of such series—for what is in the present is not an entity whose current characteristics we can describe, can talk about. What we can talk *about,* without assuming supernatural entities, is what has happened and will happen; what happens now is this *talking.* We will avoid myth in the words of our worship by refusing to try to mediate the presence of the past and future Jesus in our present state of affairs by any sort of description of the present state of affairs, by any treating of Jesus as an item thereof. In the present there is only our acting-out of the story and the act of speaking the words which bracket that act in time with the narrated story of Jesus. We talk about Jesus past and future; what is now is the deed of telling that story and enacting it as we tell it. We may put it so: In myth the word of worship is reflexive, it is *about* what happens in the act of worship itself, it attempts to state what happens in that act. This is what we must learn to do without.

That no extra describable entity is to be assumed present in our worship by no means denies the personhood of the God who is worshiped. The story of Jesus, which we narrate as a story of a past event and proclaim as future, is the story of a person. And the word which now addresses God-in-Jesus in prayer and praise is central also to secularized worship. We address God in that Jesus who lived in history and will come at the end. We address the historical figure and coming lord. We address a God who occurs for us in a person. But how can we do this now? Surely this person must be in some sense present for us to do this? Indeed. But the presence of the historical person who is also the coming lord—which presence makes it possible to address him— is not in a supernatural being who embraces both historical person and coming lord; that presence is exactly the present occurrence of the word about him and our enacting of that word. Only as part of this action does it make sense to speak to God-in-Jesus, but then it does. Here we are well back into the previous chapter.

Finally, a pair of hints about possible further elaborations of this topic. Our church architecture will have to change. We must no longer build holy lecture halls, as Protestants have done, or theater-auditoriums for viewing the sacred drama, as Catholics have done. Our space for worship must be one big stage, a space for moving and acting. Moreover, a whole aesthetic, not only of liturgical architecture, but of the sculpture, painting, etc., which should enrich that architecture and provide props for our worship-action, follows from the positions of this chapter.

In a secular age, *Christian* worship has the chance to come at last into its own. If that chance is not grasped, *worship* will cease altogether.

IV. ETHICS: WHAT IS MY NEIGHBOR?

The Last Redoubt

Let us now suppose that the demands of the previous chapters are fulfilled. Let us suppose incisive, future-giving talk about God and dramatic, unmythical worship. All can still be swallowed up by the most primitive and disastrous supernaturalism of all, which is merely that preaching and worship occur "in church" and do not emerge into the other locations of our lives, or emerge only as "implications for daily life" or something similarly unreal. Thereby the time and place we devote to preaching and worship are established as a separated supernatural sphere, no matter how antireligious and "relevant" what is said and done in that time and place may be.

This particular religious escape from God is no doubt the last and stubbornest. It is overcome only when what I do in church and what I do elsewhere hang together as one dramatically coherent story, and when what the church as a community does in its gatherings and what it does as a social and political entity also hang together. It is overcome only when what is said in church is said about life outside of church and when what is done in church is an enactment of all the joys and sorrows of secular life, and when this is so not merely in rhetoric but in fact. It is, therefore, by service to the neighbor in the world that the church and its members can make good their claim to be more than a religion.

We tell and enact the story of Jesus of Nazareth as the story of the future, and as the story of a future of which, because it will be the act of one who will judge in forgiveness, there can be predicted only its perfect newness and freedom over against all that has gone before. To live for this future is to be "open to the future," both in the sense of waiting with affirmation for whatever unpredictable time may bring, and in the sense of commitment to what must and shall be in spite of what has been and so is. It is to be a revolutionary freed of illusions about the permanent validity of his particular utopia, i.e., freed of the absolutism that makes old reactionaries out of young rebels. Thus to tell and enact the story of Jesus is to open the future for those who hear.

We will, therefore, stand up for the truth of what we say about Jesus by action that in fact opens the future, by actions that are at once assaults upon every social or personal bondage to a status quo and concrete actualizations of new and better possibilities. We will verify our talk about God, in the only way in which we can perform such a verification, by actually being open to the future—better, by living as openers of the future. Whenever—whether in our "inner" lives or in our political involvements, whether as individuals or as the church—we cling to the past, we give the lie to all our gospel-affirmations, no matter what may be the past contents to which we cling. The only desperate hope we have of talking responsibly about God, so that our hearers may feel bound even to deny what we say, is for the church to exist as a standing conspiracy against the lethargy of history, against the world's closure in the past. If we stand up for the possibility of man's having a future, then we can demand a hearing for our talk of what that future might be.

The church must be a band of spies in the service of the future. We will be using examples in this chapter; let us use one here. The "civil rights movement" began under the slogan of "integration." As this is written that slogan is being replaced by "black power." Everyone is frightened by this slogan. But perhaps believers should not be. The slogan of "integration" clearly supposed that the existing white society was to remain basically unchanged, except that the previously excluded Negroes were now to be included. The emergence of "black power" is the perception that this thoroughly conservative program is impracticable, that white society as it is is simply too moribund to accommodate anyone as alive as the Negro, that nothing less than a general social new start offers hope. Pompously offered a location a few steps higher on the white man's vision of the social ladder, those Negroes are prophets who reply, "Who needs it?"

Yet believers can also see the dominance of the past in this slogan, for it is terribly ambiguous. It could propose to freeze and glorify the present black society, or to retain the present slave-master patterns but reverse the roles. The great test of the Negro revolution will be whether it can avoid these hidden ways of clinging to the present under cover of talk about radical revolution. It seems clear what is needed: a new slogan that will carry out the revolutionary meanings of "black power" and be free of its possible reactionary meanings. The Negro church has up until now been at the heart of the movement, but only because it is the principal organization of Negro society. The test of the Negro church as a church will be its ability to spy out the future from the past and create within the movement the new language which can lead American society forward. I speak of the Negro church because the white church has long since forfeited the right to do anything here but follow.

Our example has led us to language. This is not accidental. For as it is in language that we have a future, the future-opening work of the church in society must be above all the care and creation of language, finding in each new situation of stagnation the words that can be words of hope. In our time we have developed a justified suspicion of mere words, especially from the church. The call for Christians to shut up for a time and deal in deeds instead finds response in us all. Yet the service of faith can never be entirely wordless action, for the church is the community of a story. Moreover, what the world needs is hope, and only meaningful, symbolic, word-moved action can give that. The church must be a band of those who regularly refuse to believe that nothing can be done, and are able to find the words to evoke what perhaps can be done. The church must be creative of the words that can inspire hope instead of fear.

In Europe, it is Jürgen Moltmann who has most unambiguously stated the future-opening character of what we say about God, and the consequent necessity of backing what we say by action. Christians talk about a God who is always future, who lives in his promises. The truth of our utterances is, therefore, not that they correspond to what is, but that they effectively contradict what is, that they open the possibility of making the world different. Consequently, we can interpret our utterances about God only by the call to committed work in the world.

Disturbing is the exclusive alternative. Why cannot what we say about God be *both* call to action and description true by its accuracy? To do both is hard, but if the position of this book is well taken, it is the main task of believers. Moltmann says that theology must have nothing to do with the mode of thinking of the positive sciences; particularly, historical research as a positive science must simply be overcome within theology. But should theology really be so foreign to the empirical habit of mind, its remaining years would be, I fear, few.

We have opened an unlimited field for discussion. We will follow only a few, partly arbitrarily chosen, paths through that field. There is, moreover, a preliminary task: we have first to ask how it is possible to talk at all about what we should do.

Christian Ethics

The ethical side of religion is legalism, a regulation of life based on the principle that what is to become of me is at least partly decided by what I do or do not do or am or am not with respect to a special list of behaviors or characteristics. A legalist ethic may be moralistic and contain many commands or value judgments which run counter to what we would otherwise do or seek. Or it may be libertine and exhort us to be ourselves. The difference is unimportant. Either provides us with a code—which is what is essentially religious.

A code is a definition of a way of living, a pattern for thought and action. It is a determinate and knowable body of customs, opinions, and attitudes, which provides in advance, as it were, a behavior for every occasion envisaged by the code. If the code is libertine and for certain occasions, usually sexual, stipulates

"Do as you like," this is no difference of principle. Such a coded definition of the good life is objectively given; it is my ethical task to fit myself to it. To the extent to which I succeed, I am good. To the extent I fail, I am bad. And in either case I am provided with ethical meaning for my actions.

The feature of the revolt against religion which has gained the widest acceptance is the insight that the gospel is not a code and does not even provide a code. "Situation ethics," built on Augustine's motto, "Love God and do as you will," dominates theology. Despite the fad, the insight is valid. For codes and the gospel are opposites: what codes demand, the gospel gives.

Every code demands an unending succession of things, and history produces an unending succession of codes. Which is, finally, the point codes make, for codes are the way we work out for ourselves the unending demands life makes on us. Life follows every fulfilled demand with a new one. No sooner have I begun working at honesty than I find I am expected to be self-sacrificing too. And just as I am digesting this, I am informed that it won't count unless I like it. There is no end—and that is just the point. What life finally demands is exactly that I see there is no end. What life finally demands is that I never stand still, never rest content with what I have done and am. What life—and so all codes together—finally demands is that I live for someone or something beyond myself, beyond what I have done and am. But no code provides that someone or something.

What codes only demand, the gospel, if it is true, gives, for it gives me God as the reason for my life, as the end of the story, as someone to live toward. When the gospel is told me, what all codes are really after happens: I *have* a goal beyond myself. Moreover, I have it not by my doing, but by the fact of what someone else does, that he tells me this story—here the principle of legalism is broken.

We come to a key word. The believer is *free* from any and all codes. He is free from them because he already has what they demand. There has already happened in his life what they say must happen. Therefore he no longer needs to subordinate himself to codes. He no longer needs to cram himself into the mold of a set of prearranged behaviors for all occasions, whether this be the mores of his society or the rebel code of some antisociety. The fundamental reality of the Christian life is freedom.

It is remarkable how the church has practiced Indian-giving with this. Innumerable sermons are preached on "Christian liberty"—but mostly with the same outline: "Christians are indeed free, *but* . . ." What follows the "but" depends on the denomination. In mine, "the weaker brothers," who must not be led astray by example, have been a favorite. The world population has sometimes seemed to be in two groups: weaker brothers and you and me.

It is necessary to insist: There is no code, no set of commands or principles or values or behavior patterns, which you must—or should or would be best advised to—follow in order to "be saved" or "please God" or "live a meaningful life," or be a "good" Christian. The main point that the gospel makes about our lives is that we are free from codes. You do not "have" to do anything at all for God, not even believe in him. There is no such thing as "the Christian way of life." There are as many ways of living in faith as there are believers. Any concessions made here, no matter how reasonable, will pervert the whole business of faith. The gospel is in no way sent to "uphold standards" but to liberate us from them.

The next question, of course, is: What is the content of this freedom? What are we free for? To answer this, we ask: Wherein are we free? We said that we are free in that we already have someone to live for. There is a perfectly good word for having someone to live for: "love." We are free to love—in this phrase the whole of Christian ethics is contained. It has only one maxim; I give it in my variant of Augustine's version: Love, and do what seems needed. The vagueness of the last part is essential: I am free to decide anew, not on the basis of some stated code, what in each situation is in fact needed by the one the situation gives me to love.

The gospel is permission, granting of freedom, to love. The believer is, simply, one who knows that he does not need to worry about himself because God will take care of that, and who therefore has all that time and energy unused to worry about other people.

The freedom to love is not an easy gift to receive, for freedom is a terrible boon, which men flee whenever possible. I do not want to decide for myself what shall be my life, and most surely I do not want it to be I who am responsible for the consequences of my decision. Love is also dangerous, for if I really love my neighbor, if I really commit myself to live for what he needs, I turn over some part of my life to him. Who knows what he may do with it? Especially if he is the really untrustworthy sort who most needs love? Freedom to love is hard. But it is the only authentic humanity.

However, although the insight into the situational nature of ethics is wholly correct, the way it is often handled leaves us ethically in the lurch. It has often become a refusal ever to say "This is right and that is wrong." "There are no rules in advance, we must let each new situation teach us what is to be done," is true enough. If, however, it is all we ever say, we have forgotten one very important "situation," the situation in which ethical talk is appropriate in the first place—the situation of a discussion, if only with myself, about what to do in a particular case.

If, when my neighbor says "What shall I do?" I reply only "You must use your freedom and decide for yourself," this is in most cases no help at all. This he already knew—if he had not known it he would not have asked for advice. "Decide for yourself" is usually either in effect a loveless "Don't bother me" or it is an all too religious expectation of some sort of inspiration "in the situation." When a man asks "Which way shall I turn this valve?" I do not hesitate to answer "To the right, I think." If when he asks "Shall I serve in Vietnam?" I always reply only "That you will have to decide yourself," I betray that I want to set "ethical" decisions aside into a supernatural sphere of their own distinct from our ordinary problems. What moves me to silence is that I know I have no supernatural guarantee of being right. But it is exactly the feeling that such guarantees are needed before I can speak that is the central religious delusion.

The situation of being asked what to do is itself an opportunity for loving freely. What I can do for my neighbor in this situation is take the risk of saying, very unmysteriously and knowing I may be wrong, "I think you should . . ." As we speak so with each other, we do not infringe on each others' freedom. On the contrary, it is exactly and only in such conversations that we can decide freely. I am free to make a decision only when you pose and advocate a specific alternative, for how am I to choose except from alternatives? Advocacy is exactly the help to be free that you can give me.

The first step away from religious ethics is to realize that no code has supernatural sanction. The second is to realize that concrete advice does not need supernatural sanction and that we are therefore free to give it to each other.

Such speaking is not limited to one-to-one "counseling" situations. To advocate, I must indeed know the particular situation of the individual I address. This does not, however, mean that only individual persons can be appropriately so addressed, for a group, a church, a class, or a whole society has just as particular a situation as an individual. The individuality of an individual is his particular place in history, his unique crossing of many strands of tradition. Exactly the same is true of a community. Ethical advocacy is just as much directed to some very specific situation when the partner is, for example, a city power-structure as when it is an individual. What may be said to Chicago about race will no doubt be different from what is said to an individual Chicagoan, but need not and should not be any more general or abstract. It too can have the form, "I think you should . . ."

I wish to seize this privilege and responsibility of advocacy, and discuss with you, by way of example, two areas of ethical decision, one a matter of "private" ethics, the other the matter of the policy of the church toward political and economic issues. First, however, the present discussion must go one more step: How do we find out what to advocate to each other?

"Love, and do what seems needed" is indeed the whole Christian ethical exhortation. Yet if it is to be meaningful, it must always be said in some specific explication. For this, two things are needed.

First, I must in fact be free to love. If I am not, no amount of telling me to be will help. A good bit of our ethical preachment to each other boils down to: "Be loving, damn you!" "The Christian love-ethic" is often discussed as if we were all of us bubbling springs of love needing only to find outlet. We are not. We are tied and immobilized by petty fears and minor indecisions. We have complexes, repressions, phobias, and obsessions. Worst of all, we are sinners—which means we translate everything that is said to us into a tale about ourselves and do not even hear the needs of our fellows. We are ethical vegetables: our interior life is a dim confusion in which good and evil melt together into one thin soup of "Oh, what the hell!"

If "Love, and do what seems needed" is to help, we must acquire freedom, and acquire it anew for each new occasion. For each situation in which the opportunity for love is given— i.e., in each situation where I have to do with another person— I must acquire the particular freedom to do what is needed then and there.

The gospel story gives this freedom. Therefore, "Love, and do what seems needed" gets its meaning in our lives when we say it in the course of telling the gospel. This does not mean that every ethical discussion must turn into a recital of the Creed or an evangelistic message, for what can be gospel depends itself on the situation. Indeed, the gospel gives freedom in a situation only when it is told as a story about that situation (otherwise, of course, it is not gospel anyway, no matter how often Jesus is mentioned). The gospel must be told in a particular situation as the story about how there is no need to obey the particular inhibitions which keep us from acting freely in that situation.

Second, if "Love, and do what seems needed" is to have any content, I must be able to discover what in fact my neighbor needs. This is not so simple. My neighbor himself may be quite mistaken about what is best for him. Appealed to for poison I will normally refuse. Then what if an alcoholic appeals for a drink? Yet who is to say I know better?

I can know what my neighbor needs in a given situation only if I know what he is. What he needs is what will help him on his way—but what is his way? What is his destiny? To these questions the gospel answers, for the gospel is exactly a story about the destiny of my neighbor, about what it is to be a mortal man.

Thus the gospel does not leave us in the lurch in the concrete case of decision. As we talk with each other about this man Jesus, our talk is gospel only if we do it in response to our mutual problems and choices. We talk about our lives with each other, and we try to speak as believers; that is, we try to make our ethical discussions part of our talk about Christ. Concrete exhortation to do this and not do that, ethical advocacy, is therefore simply an inevitable part of the talking we do with each other because we belong to the church.

Therefore codes too have their place. Faith is not simple absence of religion; it is the transcending of religion. Faithful ethical reflection is not the absence of codes; it is the transcending of codes. Only in the first adolescent stages of emancipation from religious tutelage is there some excuse for refusing ever to say "This is right and this is wrong." In the long tradition of the church's discussion of human life in view of the gospel, some acts have been seen to be so rarely or so generally loving that questions about them can be roughly settled in advance so as to leave us free for more serious ethical decisions. Killing, adultery, theft—only under the most extreme circumstances do these pose any ethical decision at all. Nor are these Christian commonplaces of behavior special for the believers. They are commonplaces in culture as well. This is just the point about them: The commonplace code of Christianity, for example, the Ten Commandments, does not represent the heroic demands of the life of faith. It is exactly what we should learn to follow as children and then forget about. It is utterly secular. It is a code which we use exactly because we are freed from it.

It is time to bring this abstract discussion to life by taking up a particular problem. I begin with one that seems timely.

Sex

Exactly how much and in what respects our actual sexual behavior is changing is hard to say, simply because we know little about how it used to be. Precisely the spectacular manifestations which publicists cite as proof of—depending on the viewpoint— "moral decay" or "a new honesty" are not so new and different.

Orgies have a venerable lineage, including America and including Victorian America, and it would be impossible for waitresses to wear less than they used to in St. Louis. Yet it does seem likely that our everyday sexual behavior is changing, to become little by little more like what used to be restricted to special occasions and places.

Our professed public code is clearly changing drastically. There have always been students who have held nude and promiscuous parties—but formerly they did not advertise them nor seek to have them included, as it were, in the university curricula. Although the various "free sex" publicists are an extreme case, their program does seem to represent the direction in which our public standards as a whole are moving. This direction is, on the one hand, to regard sexual activity as ethically and existentially neutral, as purely "natural." Our sexual attitudes are becoming increasingly anti-romantic.

The point, for example, of promiscuous nudity is exactly to detach sex from the specifically human, to take from it its claims to be mysterious and special. The body which is made available to general view like the body of a domestic animal is treated by its "owner" as irrelevant to whatever is the special point of human existence—and this is exactly what is intended. A woman's body that plays and teases, that is almost nude, or known to be nude but not quite visible, is a powerful existential force. "Honest" nudity, on the other hand, is humanly uninteresting unless it is private, unless the unveiling is especially for me or perhaps not meant to be seen at all.

So also wife-swapping, parties for the indulgence of "any sexual activities that don't infringe on the desires of others," or, less spectacularly, serial monogamy as a standard procedure, have the purpose of depersonalizing sex. The idea is to experience it as something which may indeed be an interpersonal activity but which is not intrinsically tied to any important personal commitments, rather like having lunch together or taking in a show. Again, the body is detached from the person: I would not allow myself to enter or be entered by a personality I do not share, but this object, "my" body, I may very well treat so.

On the other hand, our changing code makes sex more and

more important to us. Paradoxically, as we proclaim the meaninglessness of sexual activity, our behavior shows that we increasingly seek the meaning of our lives in it. We spend more and more of our time eagerly, even desperately, exposing ourselves to sexual stimuli that are less and less interesting.

The two sides of this paradoxical development can both be understood from our increasing secularism. On the one hand, as religion loses its reality, we are driven to seek the point of our existing in whatever indubitably actual "personal relations" we can find, of which sex is of course the paradigm. Yet, on the other hand, we have not gotten over the religious policy of expecting bodily activities to have meaning only by relation to some realm other than "the merely physical"—even the most blatant sex manuals always have to drag in "the spiritual significance" at the end. Thus our struggle to emancipate our actual sexual life from religious tutelage takes the form of a nihilistic insistence that sexual behavior is meaningless. Indeed, some of our deliberately perverse sexual radicalism must be seen as full-blown nihilism: "I live for sex—and sex is absurd." Nihilists work hard at meaningless sex precisely in order to destroy the last vestiges of love or hope in their lives.

The point, here as always, is not to decry secularism and try to revive a religious sex code. The decay of that code makes average satisfactory sexual virtue rarer, and true sexual virtue, when achieved, all the more authentic. One simply pays the price of the other. Nor is it the point to adapt ourselves to the new libertine code. We are as free from that code as from any other. Yet the situation in which we have to act freely is the society defined by this code, with its problems and possibilities. It is in it that we have to find the ways to love freely, with our bodies and their remarkable pairing arrangements.

The word by which we live, here also, is: "Love, and do what seems needed." Therefore, the question is: When the neighbor in question is a possible sexual partner in one or another degree, what is the concretion of this word? What does the gospel tell me about what it means to be human sexually? And so about what this neighbor needs from me? What are the specific sexual freedoms of the gospel? What are our resources for decision?

It is my neighbor's body I am concerned with (that this is not an unloving or crude characterization of the situation is part of what we have to learn from the gospel). The gospel says that he or she will "rise" in that body; that is, the gospel says that the fulfillment of my neighbor's life will not be a purely "spiritual" event—whatever that might be—it will be a meeting with the person Jesus of Nazareth, and will therefore be something done and experienced as the body, for the body is our presence to each other—there is obviously no communion of persons which is not a bodily communion. Sight and sound are, after all, quite as physical as touch. The story my neighbor will enact with Christ on that last day will be the story, not of some special religious and soulish sort of deeds, but of the actual occurrences of life, of what happened with his or her body. Our histories, the stories of our challenges and responses to each other, are precisely the stories of our bodies. At least, so says the gospel, which names the denouement of our stories "the resurrection of the body."

Thus what happens to my neighbor's body is never ethically or theologically indifferent. Even if we try, our reality as persons cannot be separated from the empirical events of our bodies' histories, for our reality as persons will be posited by our last future—and that will be "resurrection of the body." By every touch, by every intrusion or permission, I co-author with my neighbor an incident in the story he or she will reinterpret with Christ.

What then does my neighbor need from me? We need from each other bodily life that is clearly and definitely identical with our lives as *persons*, with our lives as those called to a future fulfillment. We need that we treat each other as persons, and that we do not in any way distinguish our use of each other's bodies from this personal relation.

Personal life is life by words; it is hearing and responding to promises and challenges. Every caress should be a word addressed to this neighbor, a call or promise to his or her hopes and fears and dreams, and be given in the expectation of a response which will appeal in turn to my future. If the caress cannot be given so, it should not be given at all—for it will be a lie, a curse, an acted-out "Damn you!" Most certainly, neither force nor psychological manipulation nor acquiescence in manipulation can ever be appropriate. Only what can occur in honest and free address and response can even come into question as what this neighbor might need from me, as a possible sexual deed of love. Love can never call us to treat a neighbor as a sort of elaborate masturbation apparatus—not even when the misuse would be mutual.

What does this neighbor need? We need faithfulness. All words, all addresses of one person to another, are promises; they give the one addressed the right to expect something. If our caresses are words, if they are part of our lives as persons, then they too are promises. Every caress is either a promise or what ought to be a promise—i.e., a lie—and if both partners understand that the promise is not meant, this only means that both are liars. What a particular caress promises can only be known in the situation when giving it becomes a possibility, and will in fact always be known if we only remember *that* it will be a promise. There will be some caress which is a last promise, a promise of permanence. To explore my neighbor's body or to allow mine to be explored is either a promise of faithfulness or it is a blasphemy, a burlesque and renunciation of the meaning of life.

What does this neighbor need? We have said that we need bodily life that is personal. Vice versa, we need personal life that is bodily. He or she needs to learn and rehearse joy and sorrow, anticipation and remembrance, as joy at, sorrow over, anticipation of, and remembrance of bodily life. He or she can learn to await the resurrection of the body with joy and see it as the fulfillment of life, by learning from me the glee and sport of the body and its extraordinary arrangements. There are, however, many ways for two people to teach this to each other, and it is necessary to remember that one of the most vital ways is by *not* becoming sexual partners.

We take one more step in this analysis. Since sexual union is a promise of permanent devotion of two people to each other, it creates a new social unit, whether we will or no. The way in which we have proceeded so far, as if the two possible partners were the only people on earth, is an arbitrary and unreal abstraction. Who is this neighbor? A member, perhaps, of the church, certainly a member of a family, a class, a city, a nation, a race. To ask what can be my deed of love for him or her is also to ask what can be my deed of love to his or her family, church, and society. When the gospel tells us to practice our bodily existence with gusto, it frees us from the delusion that sexual life is a mysterious, inward, privatist matter. Then we are free to admit what is obvious, that sexuality is precisely a matter of *bodies,* which means of all the elaborate web and history of our communications with each other, of the social processes and institutions by which we live. Whose business is it what we two do? Practically everybody's! It is, in fact, exactly as much your business as it is ours. The claims of society can be evaded only by an evasion of reality so infantile as to be, perhaps, past the reach of persuasion or argument and in the realm of coercive law, however unmodish such an idea may be.

In particular, the new social unit created by love can only be a unit of the real society to which we two belong—not of some other society we *wish* were real. This means, first, that concealment of the existence of the relation is essentially inappropriate. It means, second, that the social and legal arrangements which our society provides for permanent sexual devotion are the only ways through which the new human entity we create can be real. What does my neighbor need from me? He or she needs to create with me—or someone else!—a real new "one flesh," not a child's pretense.

If "Love, and do what seems needed" is to be meaningful, we must, we said, be able to discover what our neighbor needs. We also said that we must acquire the particular freedom to love required. We go on to this: What am I free from here?

I am free from codes. I do not need to lose my love because some code says it is forbidden—though I may very well be called to say goodbye to a partner who is not my love, or one who is. Nor need I make him or her my partner because a libertine code says I must.

I am also free from the gods and demons behind these codes.

I need not necessarily obey the interiorized voice of my parents called the conscience—my parents and so my conscience can err. Nor need I obey the great god "They."

I need not obey Eros and Aphrodite. The story of my neighbor's body does not lead straight to resurrection without interruption. Since my partner will die, eternal fulfillment is not inherent in his or her bodily existence; it will come only by the miracle of resurrection. Thus the demands of my neighbor's body are not infallible. I need not obey "Love" or "Sincerity," for it is not so that "love" in the sense of glands and sentiment can justify everything done in its name, nor that being "sincere" is an absolute—most fools are sincere.

What am I free from? I do not need to prove anything, neither my masculinity nor my freedom from bourgeois standards, nor my rectitude, nor my self-control, nor that I am not a legalist. For it is already settled how I will be judged at last—nothing is left to prove.

I am, finally, free from supernatural bondage to my genitalia. When my body becomes an object to me, as it tends to at present, then it or some part of it can become special, lordly, sacrosanct—a supernatural being. Many men spend years of their lives as life-support and transportation systems for their penises. Many women spend their years as exhibition backgrounds for their breasts and buttocks. There is no need for such undignified and mechanistic slavery. We do not need any experience that badly, for we have been given a point to our lives which can survive the loss of anything at all. A good many other men and women are in the polar form of the same bondage, trying to pretend they have no genitalia. Some frantic libertines are really of this sort. There is no need for this slavery either—the thing is there, enjoy it.

Given our culture, these considerations will lead the believer to a code, a code of permanent monogamy inaugurated by the first full sexual relation. This result will no doubt be disappointing to many—it is so stodgy, unoriginal, and unenforceable. Two things can be said: First, the originality of the gospel is not primarily in the inventing of interesting new codes, but in freedom from codes, including this one. Sometimes reflection in a specific situation on what the gospel tells us about human life will lead to the demand for a new code, sometimes not. It is not a virtue in itself for a code to be new and different. Second, it is only in the first, romantic, still secretly religious, stage of the revolt against religion that we think that all established order must be overthrown. A genuinely secular attitude is characterized by calm and pragmatism.

The Church as Pressure Group

Our second case of ethical reflection is very different. Here the ethical subject is not an individual, but the church, the community as such. We ask: How shall the church comport itself as an economic, social, and political influence?

Whether or not to exercise this influence is not a choice given the church. Because the church is the fellowship gathered around the story of the man Jesus, and because it possesses that story only by the usual processes of historical tradition, the church is a social, economic, and legal entity whether its members want it to be or not. It is bodies, not disembodied souls, that gather. The church must also make provision for the perpetuation of its story; i.e., it must organize its gatherings. As an existent and functioning social entity, the church will affect social institutions and decisions. The only question is how.

The church is called to be the salt of the earth. It is called to be a standing center of revolution against all stagnation, against society's inclination to close itself against the future. The church is also called to bind up wounds, the wounds which result from the world's battle against time. In a worldly culture, the chief such wound is its false spiritual life, its inevitable fraudulent religion. If we put these together, we may say that the present great social task of the church is to debunk false supernaturalism and seek to alleviate the suffering it creates, to fight civic religiosity.

It is a hard calling God has given the West at this climax of its story—the calling to live without illusions. It is hard to have no gods to share the blame, to know that life's meaningfulness has

no guarantee other than the hidden God. Apart from the story
of Christ, we will always shrink from so naked a confrontation
with truth into some degree of illusion. If genuine religion is not
possible, we will by ourselves certainly fall victim in some degree to false religion.

In culture, of course, everything is a matter of degree. Although faith's kind of fidelity to truth is not wanted, neither is it
needed, and a sanity and clarity sufficient for the daily tasks is
possible. The world will not attain the escape from illusion
which is by faith alone, but it can attain pragmatism in politics,
a plurality of schools in the arts, at least the pursuit of objec-
tivity in science, and tolerable economic and social justice. The
great danger is that our century will recoil completely from the
secular reality it has evoked and fall total victim to the accom-
panying inauthentic religion. Our governments may become
divinely ordained by ersatz divinities, our science "socialist" or
"democratic," our arts illustrations of artificially sacrosanct
values. The church's service to the world is to help prevent this.

The church must be the implacable social and political foe
of all pseudo-religion, especially the Christian sort. Since the
eye of faith will be able to track down the winding subtleties of
religious quackery, this is our job on behalf of our brothers. When
phony religion is found in cultural power, the church must attack. Any compromise would be a pact with demons.

As this is written, the Vietnamese war is escalating. The need
for the debunking of pseudo-religion is so pressing in this case
that I cannot choose any other to illustrate my point, even
though the situation to which I directly speak may be past by
the time anyone reads this. What I have to do, therefore, is
limit my discussion to what is certainly now true and will be true
no matter how the war develops, or which side of the present
debates may later be taken to have been right.

We fight, we are told, to "stop Communism." But if there
were such a being as a "Communism" that could be "stopped" it
would be a supernatural being. Among beings of the ordinary
sort, there are Communists, Communist governments and parties,
and no doubt Communist plots. Very likely some of these are

indeed very wicked. "Communism," however, is either merely a more or less useful label for a broad group of social, political, and intellectual phenomena, which is not the sort of thing that can be "stopped," or it is the name of a supposed great spirit "behind" all these phenomena, i.e., of a supposed devil-god. Insofar as we do what we do in order to "stop Communism," we are placating a presumed deity; we are devotees of a pseudo-religion.

It is belief in this one great demon prowling the world that makes us react in one stereotyped way to every political development we take for one of his epiphanies, which has made us treat the crises in Greece, Berlin, Cuba, the Dominican Republic, and Vietnam as if they were all the same, whereas they were alike in almost no important respect. There is no such demon—and it is a political task of the church, of the community of those freed by faith from any need for ersatz religion, to shout this from the housetops, and to exert whatever weight it has to counter policies originating in his cult.

We urgently need to be freed from such superstition. We need to recover our freedom to examine each political crisis or opportunity as it arises and on its own merits, without being precommitted to the belief that everything that happens in the world is a manifestation either of "Communism" or of "Democracy" (with the capital, another myth). When President Johnson and secretaries McNamara and Rusk lump together all international confrontations from Munich on, and summon us to a crusade against some mysterious evil essence that is supposed to be the same in all these cases, one hopes desperately that this is mere cant for mass consumption, that there are other and more rational reasons for our actions. But the horrid suspicion grows that our leaders believe this childish superstition, and that their belief and that of other leaders before them is a main factor in our policy decisions. It is possible that there are rational reasons for our intervention, but if there are they are being kept secret—perhaps because the public is not interested.

Besides a devil-god, our foreign policy has a salvation, "Victory." Perhaps as the particular war in Vietnam develops, we will sooner or later have attained something we can persuade ourselves is victory or will have given up for this time. However, Victory in the abstract—or its synonym for Vietnam, "self-determination"—is our goal at the time I write, and the damage to American life of pursuing yet another fanaticism is being done.

"Victory" is exactly like religious "salvation" in that we cannot ever say exactly what would have to happen to be "Victory"; at best we operate with poetic images and analogies. As a war aim, "Victory" is therefore a murderous fanaticism, for neither we nor our opponents can ever be sure we have attained it, and can therefore only fight on until someone is annihilated or "surrenders unconditionally." Already our war aims of World War II were fanatic. We sacrificed entire populations to "Unconditional Surrender," and finished with the whole burnt offering of Hiroshima and Nagasaki, whereupon much of mankind quite justifiably concluded we were a nation to fear and mistrust.

Those who have heard that God has suffered for all men do not support absolutized war aims like "Victory" or "Freedom" or "Self-Determination." If we take the responsibility of killing our brothers, surely we do this only in the most extreme circumstances and as the only alternative to yet greater evils. Therefore, only wars fought for rigidly limited and carefully defined aims can possibly be supported by the church and individual believers (and not all of these). We must never be religious about war. Insofar as our Vietnamese adventure lacks such aims, it is indefensible. It should be the responsibility of the church at the time of this writing to point this out in every available forum, to use what influence it has to oppose the intervention until it is made clear exactly what limited goods we are seeking to accomplish, and meanwhile to give succor to all those who suffer from our intransigence. If when this is read, reasonable war aims have been defined, we may be very grateful.

The church's duty to give succor brings me to the other part of the church's special social task. Every false religion is a distortion of reality and therefore hides some part of the world of men from its devotees—as the people we tag "Communists" are invisible to us. Whenever we are possessed by a demon, some of our fellow men simply escape our view, and so also our ordinary social means of help and protection. For decades, the majority society of America did not see our Negro population because of the myth of White Protestant America. For decades, we did not see our culturally self-replacing poor because of the myths of Unlimited Opportunity and Postwar Prosperity. Because the church is here to be the social reality of those whose eyes are cleared of such phantasms, it has as its special task to seek out and succor those who, because society does not see they are there, will not otherwise be succored.

Until Michael Harrington pointed it out, the subculture of the poor was invisible to us. Now it is, if anything, too much scrutinized, having become a major partisan concern, yet we may wonder if it is the poor or only The Poor who have become so visible. The new visibility of Negro Americans is so great that one actually feels the skin-color of our city crowds has somehow changed overnight, but Negroes are still not very visible to the holders of economic power in northern cities. And those American Indians who remain in cultural groups are still behind the walls we built to keep them out of sight.

Other groups than those defined by class or race or economics can be forgotten. As an example, let me mention a group which has been created exactly by our secular culture and its phony religion. I tag them the "quiet fanatics," hoping by giving them a tag to make them visible. These come from the thousands of good people, mostly in small towns and the countryside, who are still basically religious in an authentic way, who live, if you will, in the 19th century. Many of them are unable to distinguish the real but inchoate religious intuitions of their hearts from the propaganda of the ersatz religions. These are loving people who nevertheless hate and fear Negroes and Jews, because, for example, the *Defender* has convinced them that the NAACP and "the Jews" are in league with Communism to destroy "Christian America." They are pious people who are bereft of the comfort of the life of their denominations because, to use examples from my denomination, *Lutherans Alert* or *The Morning Glory* has told them its pastors and teachers are apostate to "Modernism."

They are generous people who vote against every candidate who supports necessary welfare programs because radio evangelists have made them see these as tools of "Bible-denying liberals" seeking to undermine the supposed Protestant dogma of "Individual Initiative."

Although these people are not fanatics and do not join anti-Communism crusades or initiate petitions to fire their integrationist pastors, their lives are distorted quite as sadly as if they were. They are victims. My present point is that nobody tries to help them because they are invisible. The mythology of the liberals assumes that all with such opinions are fanatics. The reactionaries find them halfhearted. Their denominations too do nothing to free them of their tormentors, because that would disturb the great and mighty god, "The Peace of the Church"—though the church of Jesus Christ, on the other hand, could help them in their misery.

Finally, *how* shall the church exercise its political and economic influence? By exactly the same means as any other group, for the service of the church to the world is not a religious undertaking. The public activity of the church is an undertaking in our common life with all the reasons and pressures that decide what is done there. Of these reasons and pressures the valid reasons and legitimate pressures together are what used to be called "reason." The church will exercise its social influence by reason.

Insofar as effective channels of public debate and persuasion are available, we should use them. When we argue in such forums for what should or should not be done by society, we should bring no special religious justifications for our views. To label a course of action "Christian" or "unchristian" cuts, here, no ice at all. Even if for cultural reasons it would be effective for the church to argue in this way, it should refrain, for the gospel adds no ethical directives whatever to those which can be discovered in the ordinary course of our living together. There is no "new law" special for Christians, nor are there any political or economic policies supportable only by arguments drawn from Christian theology. When the church appears in public debate, it brings forward reasons and seeks points of persuasion which would be available to anyone if they could only see them.

Insofar as those rather less public channels by which most of our political decision is influenced are available to the church, we should use them too. "Politics" may well be a dirty business, but so is life. Also in this forum, the considerations we will have to urge will not be specific to the religious.

This does not mean that the gospel has nothing to say about our political and economic life. If it did not, such discussions as those of this chapter would be illegitimate. We may very well have theological reasons for the policies we advocate; it is only that these are irrelevant to our advocacy itself. Our discussion within the church as to what public course to take should definitely be theological.

The question behind all this is *how* the gospel guides our social thinking. The gospel works in the world of politics not by adding directives to those adducible by reason, but by freeing us from unreason, by freeing us from prejudices and myths. There is no such thing as enlightened self-interest, and that is just the permanent trouble with society. We are irrational in our conduct of our life together because each of us is deafened by his terror for his own life. The believer is freed of this terror.

The gospel frees us of unreason in this way: As we learn to speak the gospel to others and to ourselves, we learn a new language. We learn a language in which it is possible to speak of goals and purposes without using the myth-words that distort our perceptions of the world. We learn to speak a language whose forms can be used without assuming the existence of gods or demons. For as we speak about Jesus of Nazareth as the point of our lives, we learn a language of history. We learn to measure existent states of affairs and proposed alternatives not against changeless perfect entities and changeless embodiments of evil, but by pragmatic criteria. We learn to seek the meaning of our lives not in conformity to a code, but in their dramatic coherence, in the way in which our various means and ends make a story.

Believers do not, then, have special criteria for their choices.

What we do have is the freedom—not all at once but in each particular situation—to see what everyone could see, to use the common criteria.

Therefore it is also to be expected that from time to time believers will choose otherwise than do other men of their society. In our present situation, it is, to stay with our examples, to be expected that believers will show other patterns of sexual behavior and support other international policies than do many. Yet this is not because we have ethical directives they cannot hear, but precisely because we do not. If we choose untypically, it is not because we are religious, but because we are worldly and the world is religious.

When believers do choose differently than does the dominant sector of society, and when their choice proves annoying to society—as it often will—what then? We have no call to exacerbate the conflict for its own sake, for we are not trying to prove anything, least of all how different we are. If God wills to bring through us not peace but a sword, that is his business. *We* are to be peacemakers. Neither have we any cause to shrink from conflict, for we have nothing to lose. Our call is to forceful and clearheaded advocacy by whatever means are coherent with the policy we advocate. The chips may fall where they will.

If they fall wrong, we may have to suffer, which will be our last means of political and economic presence. Passive resistance, i.e., suffering, will not come naturally to believers, for we are neither Buddhists nor masochists. It should, however, come when needed, for if we suffer by advocating the common good, so did Jesus. This is not the only or most helpful description of what he did, but surely it is one. There is, of course, nothing especially "Christian" about such suffering. The jails of Mississippi make strange cellmates. Even Christ's suffering was not of some special religious variety. In the advocacy of the common good, whoever will join is our brother.

Large parts of the ethical policy recommended here are evidently very similar to the stance advocated by Harvey Cox. Let me first say that I agree jubilantly with almost the entire concrete content of *The Secular City*, above all with its affirmation of the city and its impersonality and creativity. Yet criticism of this gloriously written tract is much needed.

I share the usual criticism that Cox's ethical attitude lacks a theological basis. In themselves, of course, ethical recommendations need no theological reasons. But a tract written to persuade the church that it should adopt certain ethical recommendations does need theological reasons for why the church should adopt these instead of others. It remains quite mysterious *why* we should live as Cox wants, or what might make it possible to do so.

The lack of a theological basis results, I think, from a definite theological error. Cox identifies the secular city and the City of God, the penultimate and the ultimate, the "law" and the "gospel." There is in him no hint that if the truly secular city were attained, the Kingdom of God would still be future. When this identification is made, only two alternatives open: One can forget about ultimate fulfillment as a judge over all historically actualizable programs, and simply be an ethical humanist; or one will wax theological and ultimately-concerned about one's politics, etc. Cox has chosen the second path, and so has ironically not developed a secular ethical policy, but a thoroughly religious one.

V. STRUCTURE: PROCLAMATION AND CONSPIRACY

The Shape of Congregational Life

For the life of faith, whether of an individual or of a community, to be as I have described it, will require that the whole structure of church life change. As it is now, neither gathering for worship around the story of Jesus nor service to the neighbor in the world is taken with final seriousness. Instead, the energy of our faith is directed into a specially created religious sphere between the two—the sphere of "church work," or of one or another "apostolate," or of "the implications of the gospel for daily life." This special reality is a typical piece of supernature; the way in which the church goes at its life is fundamentally religious.

As our church life is now structured, when we gather for worship we come under the assumption that this event has no final value in itself, that the point is to "get something from it" for "life," which is thus assumed to be lived elsewhere. This assumption is then unfailingly reinforced by what we hear during worship, where we are regularly told that all our praying, etc., will not count unless we *really* believe" or "commit ourselves" or something, which is to be proved by our behavior on "the other six days of the week."

Yet when we then turn to the other six days of the week, and to our family life, work, and civic responsibilities, we are not set free. Rather, what we do is allowed to count as the required life of faith only if it somehow ties explicitly back to religion: if it "leads people to Christ" or "shows God's love" or at least is done in a bloc with other church members as a church project. For the most part, the works which are supposed to be the reality of our worshiping do not get even this far out into the world, and we settle for ushering or serving on the church finance committee or attending church organizations.

Thus the life of faith comes to be neither a life of worship nor a life of service in the world, but something in between, a life of "religious activity," for which the story of Jesus told in worship is supposed to provide the motivation and the world the opportunity. The church is fundamentally structured as what we now call an agency, an organization which makes itself available for the facilitation of one or another desirable activity. In the case of the church, we have a sort of omnibus agency for whatever social, philanthropic, or business projects can be captured to provide a religious sphere of activity.

The main endeavor of this agency is to maintain itself over against other agencies, for it is not at all clear that the church agency has any unique task, other than self-perpetuation, which agencies of government, private philanthropy, or the academic community do not or at least could not also do. The church exists as a sphere of thought and work arbitrarily carved out of life and set up as the life of faith by tagging it with words drawn from the life of worship. "Devotions" at beginning and end are supposed to make a religious occasion out of anything from the often cold-blooded deliberations of a denominational investment committee to a quiet afternoon ladies' coffee party. Indeed, the content of the religious sphere is irrelevant. All that counts is that *some* activities or other be reserved for the church, so that a religious sphere shall subsist.

This structure obtains both locally and at the denominational level. At the local level, one proves that he is a good member of his congregation by participating in one or another of its organizations. These organizations for the most part accomplish nothing but their own perpetuation, which is all, rhetoric aside, that they are intended to do, for thereby a certain segment of life is cut out for the church and the religious sphere is established. That one could do crafts or gossip under other auspices is clear; but here it counts as a bit of religion.

At the denominational level, it is not so immediately apparent what is wrong with this pattern, for the church agency often in fact accomplishes a good deal at this level. Great social, philanthropic, and educational projects are successfully carried out. But the relation of all this to the gospel is tenuous. When the church bureaucracy tries to act in a specifically believing way, it usually becomes trivial and ridiculous; whereas what it does well is usually something that could just as well be done by any other agency.

The rise of a secular society is the church's great opportunity to overcome this self-conception as the agency devoted to the religious sphere, to escape the location into which it has fallen between the two proper poles of its life. In a secular society, the church should be forced to recast itself, for there is no hope of its maintaining its agency function. Every development of our society appropriates to secular agencies some function previously left to the religious sphere. We no longer need our congregations to be centers of community life, nor do we need our denominations to feed our poor or educate our children or send hospitals to Africa. The desperate position of the church in this regard is shown by the marvel that it is often religious people who argue against the political interests of the poor and suffering, on the grounds that the welfare state threatens to leave the church with nothing to do. A radical recasting can be evaded only if the church is willing to do redundantly exactly the same things that are being done anyway by other segments of society, under the pretense that, let us say, a relief project which would in any case have been carried out becomes a religious activity because it is administered by clergymen. If the church were to take this way—as it shows every sign of doing—it would move from being an agency for religious affairs to being an agency for *ersatz* religious affairs, in depressing correlation to the pattern we have marked generally.

What then *should* the structure of the church be? The church should be a gathering for worship and a conspiracy against the inertia of society. It should be both as radically as possible, and without creating special functions and activities in between the two to provide an out from both.

Insofar as the church is a gathering for worship, the structure of congregational life must make it plain that this gathering neither has nor needs any purpose beyond itself, that we do not need to get anything out of it and that whether it attracts new members or helps raise the budget is irrelevant. We do not worship to live; we live to worship, which does not need to mean that we go about our business filled with some sort of longing for a "worship experience," but simply that when we go to hear about Jesus and pray in his name we go to do this and need no further reasons.

As the place of mutual ethical advocacy and as a force in public life, the church should be structured as a cell, as a standing conspiracy ready to be mobilized by any of its members who sees a need. Since the church has no permanent special functions in society, but rather watches for the continuously new forms of society's false religiosity and for the continuously new injustices created thereby, the work of the church in the world must always be *ad hoc.* A believer who thinks he sees a developing social stagnation, or a case of hidden suffering, should be able to summon a gathering of his fellow believers for deliberation and action, whether it be of two friends to cook a meal, of a nation's bishops—or whatever we have—to make a public statement or to put pressure on a government, of the believers in a neighborhood to supply workers for a doorbell-ringing campaign against block-busting, or of people with a common problem—perhaps members of a profession—to advise each other. Nor should this action be the responsibility of special permanent organizations. The conspiratorial meetings of the church should be gathered just as are its meetings for worship; indeed, often they will be the same meetings.

The life of the church must thus be carried not by organs of the organization—boards, committees, etc.—but by various general and special gatherings of the community. For examples: The ladies' auxiliary should be allowed to die, or turn into the club for the lonely that it might usefully be. What is needed instead is that in a residential community there be someone with a list of trusty women who can always be rallied to give the help social agencies do not, or that the believing teachers in a school system threatened by flight from racial integration be able to find and support each other in commitments to stay and fight, and in the joint search for new ideas. Permanent "Bible classes" may or may not be needed; but there is great need of opportunity for believers to talk with each other about a new book of social criticism or popular theology, with people present who are informed in the relevant fields.

The moral phenomenon of these years is the rebirth of ethical and intellectual enthusiasm in the service of love—outside the church. The very people who sit sadly in church from a sense of inherited duty, and can no longer be moved to commit their time and energies to the youth group or the mission society, respond with glad hearts to the call of the Urban League or VISTA, where they join a living community with those who were never in the church or who have long since left it. The point is not somehow to try to "reclaim" this vitality for religion—the church should never want to "reclaim" anything; its hope is in the future. The point is to recognize this diaspora gladly as the very reality of the church, to work out structures whereby the scattered spies for the future can recognize and help each other, and to learn to do worship around the story of Jesus as our celebration together of the future for which we work.

The Ministry

There are many things that will have to change to make possible a congregational life so structured. We choose two for discussion. The first will be the ministry.

There is no reason why every group of Christians who regularly worship and conspire together should be defined or organized on the same plan. A student congregation defined by where or even what they study, or an industrial congregation defined by the plant, are fully as appropriate as a congregation defined by where its members sleep. So also the ministry of one kind of congregation should not necessarily be structured like that of a different kind of congregation. Clearly, the present uniformity, where there is always "the pastor" as the chief incumbent of all the congregation's ministries, with the rest of the ministerium composed of his assistants, ordained or lay, is outdated. Indeed, the one thing that can probably be said of all congregations of whatever sort is that if in this time they want to be more than agencies for religion, they will need many ministers, not one.

A general agency for religious matters is quite properly organized as a volunteer society under the control of its members and run by a general executive, "the pastor." But if we define the life of the congregation as worship and revolution, and so define the ministry by what is to be *done,* then we will need many ministries. Then we will need some to take various roles in worship, some to scout the economy, some to preach, some to heal, some to prod the local community action program, etc.

Emphatically, this does not mean that the congregation needs to hire additional seminary graduates as "assistant pastors," on the "minister of music" or "youth minister" pattern. In most congregations, it will no doubt be desirable for one or two of the ministers, especially of the preachers, to be theologians. For these, the congregations will usually turn to graduates of theological schools—though by no means necessarily and perhaps decreasingly as theology ceases to be esoteric. But for most ministerial functions, university or seminary theological training is unnecessary. Every ministry has its theology; working this out for each ministry will be the joint task of those involved in it and the professional theologians in the ministerium, whose chief task will be to help their colleagues in theological reflection about their work. So also those ministers whose peculiar service is such theological reflection will be free to be genuinely professional theologians; and the seminaries and divinity schools will be free to be schools of theology, instead of the trade schools for religious executives which they now are.

For the most part, the ministerium should be recruited from the congregation itself. The minister who celebrates the Eucharist need not be one of those in the full-time employ of the congregation, if there are any; he need not be the preacher; nor need he always be the same man. He should be a member chosen from the congregation for imagination, freedom, and the judgment needed to admit or exclude from the table; and learned in the performance, traditions, and theology of the liturgy, for which he need by no means go off to seminary. And there should be as many others ordained to special liturgical functions as there are such functions. So also as a congregation responds to the special opportunities for service which its particular situation presents, it must find those of its people able to lead these tasks, ordain them to their work, and within the ministerium help them to the particular kinds of theological maturity needed for their various ministries.

The ministers must each be absolutely independent of the mass of the church in their various assignments, short of removal by the ministerium. The call comes from men, but the office which serves the telling and interpretation of the gospel is established by God.

It is evident that the generality of the church is not going to take the stance in the world advocated here. The church presently functions as a shelter for those suffering from religious nostalgia. If its work is to be controlled by its general constituency, it will neither worship nor serve, for the religiously nostalgic can neither understand nor even be interested in the true life of the church. They are, indeed, its bitterest social opponents. Even should social upheaval—or a sudden decision of the preachers to preach the gospel—free the church from its burden of the irrelevantly attached, it is hard to imagine how even the most purified church could ever do the church's true work as a mass. For living worship requires creativity, the church's work in the world consists of creativity, and the creative will be few in any society. The church is the liberated society, but the work in which liberty is real will always be done for all by a few.

Therefore, those who carry the preaching and enacting of the gospel should be as independent of the church public as possible. A believer concerned to fight racial injustice should be free to get on with his work and to recruit any who can and will work with him. In his place, he is the church; and whether the majority of the church public support him is irrelevant. The main purpose of the political structure of the church should be to make this evident to believers and unbelievers and to guard him against interference from the foot-draggers.

If the ministerium were organized and expanded as we suggest, this freedom would be especially important for its members. But in general, the church should have the political structure of a liberal society in the classical sense. However inapplicable the principle may be in society as a whole that everyone should be free to do what does not clearly harm the general welfare, it fits the church perfectly, if we define general welfare as the intelligibility and believability of the gospel. This does not necessarily mean we must govern the church democratically; a thoroughly monarchical episcopate may be just what is needed. Finally, as things are now, our only hope is in the initiative and even defiance of the individual who takes up the church's work where he sees it undone, whether anyone else has ordained him to it or not.

Parish Education

Without doubt, the part of its life to which the usual congregation devotes the most effort, and where its failure is most complete, is education. Let us state it flatly at the beginning: The usual accomplishment of the system of Sunday school, weekday released time school, baptism or confirmation instruction, and daily vacation Bible school is to teach children that Christianity is trivial, dull, and demoralizing.

Parish education is now an elaborate effort to indoctrinate with a metaphysic and a morality. Where the gospel has been most diluted, the metaphysic is a sort of pantheist personalism for suburbia, a doctrine of the eternal significance of the nice guy. Elsewhere, the metaphysic is dualistic. On the one hand there is the sweet-Jesus ontology, transcendentalized sentimentality; on the other hand, there is "God," who "made everything." We leave it to the poor students to do a vulgarized recapitulation of the trinitarian controversies and put them together. The morality is straight chamber of commerce, leavened with pity-the-poor-Negro. It is where the Bible comes in: "Abraham gave Lot first choice. Do we give our friends first choice?"

Most of us finally reject these implausible teachings, if not consciously, and with them all too often the gospel. Of course, it would be still worse to believe them. The difficulty is in the very foundation of our educating: the assumption that there is a body of religious information, analogous to geographical or arithmetical information, and that it is the responsibility of the church to communicate this information and inculcate the appropriate corresponding attitudes. But while there may of course be such a subject matter, it is no part of the church's mission to cultivate it, at least not in the secular epoch.

Society has trapped the church into doing the alien job of inculcating society's religion. In a secular society this is phony religion, which makes the assignment all the more foreign to the church and results in the kind of theological education we just described. The church must free itself from this imposition.

So far as the church is concerned, there is no independent body of religious knowledge. What there is, is on the one hand actual life in the telling and enforcing of the gospel, and on the other hand theology, that is, reflection on what to say and do in carrying out this life. Theology does not form an independently communicable body of information; it is always relative to the actual preaching, worshiping, and serving of the church. The theological reflection which any particular believer needs to do, is what pertains to performing his part in the church's life. The educational task of the congregation is to initiate individuals into the life of the community and throughout their life in that community facilitate their understanding of what they are doing. The church has nothing at all in which to educate those who do not share in its life.

As soon as we see that the church has no call to provide a school system to teach some extra subject that the other schools cannot cover, we will be free to dismantle the whole creaking affair. There is indeed much learning and thinking that must be fostered in the congregation. But the system of religious education fosters these hardly at all.

We must be entirely clear that we cannot in any way educate people into faith. The church's education must presuppose the address of the gospel and life in the church, just as the educating which society at large does presupposes humanity and membership in the society in question. What we have to accomplish can then be clearly defined: we have to teach people what to do as members of the church; and we have to help them do this humanly, with understanding and with the possibility of creativity that understanding opens. Our principle must be that the learnings and problems for reflection which the congregation presents to its members must be those they need for each particular part of the life of the church as they are inducted into it.

There is, of course, a knowledge of the gospel story and of what is done in worship, and a generally informed alertness to society, which must be the common possession of all believers. For adult converts, these should be inculcated by a period of apprenticeship in worship and regular instruction by theologians and the socially aware in the parish, like the catechumenate of the ancient church. The children of believers should be brought up in this knowledgeableness step by step. Nobody can really do this but the parents, and the entire responsibility must simply be returned to them.

This last proposal will meet strong objections. It will be said that many parents refuse to assume this responsibility. This is true, but it is time to recognize and make plain that those who refuse this responsibility thereby resign from the church, and that while the church has everything to say to those who are not yet part of its life, it has nothing in which to *educate* them. It is only because we suppose that what the church has to teach is religious knowledge useful independently of life in the church, and further suppose that we are saved by religion—whether by "saved" we mean adjusted to life, or rescued from degradation, or gotten into heaven—that it is intolerable to think of excluding anyone and that we think we have to set up a school system for any whose parents deign to send them.

In general, if I may digress, the way to meaningful church discipline will be recognition of what the church in fact can and cannot do. If the church is a religious society and if religion is a good thing, then it is cruel to exclude anyone. If the church saves its members, then the more the better. But if we recognize that it is God who saves, then making reasonable demands for practicing commitment to the actual work of the church judges no one's position before God and excludes no one from anything that can do him any good. It only says: If you want to work at telling and enacting the story about Jesus, and at conspiring in his name, fine; if you don't, you don't. It does not exclude from the final destiny the gospel gives, only from the gatherings of those committed to it. Those outside the gathering are exactly the ones to whom the gathering has to speak the gospel and of whom, therefore, the gospel's promises are true.

It will also be objected that many parents are unable to teach their children. This brings us to the other side of the congregation's educating. For all aspects of the congregation's life, opportunity should be provided and enforced for discussion, practice, lectures, reading, or whatever seems appropriate for those entering or at work there. Believing parenthood is exactly such a special work in the church and demands its particular theologizing. No doubt our parents do not know what to tell their children, but they can learn—and here is one of the places where the congregation should indeed establish classes and curricula.

Precisely what special educational undertakings a congregation should make depends on its situation. One that might be important for many situations would be something like a choir school for all ages. Here those responsible for the congregation's life of worship should work and perhaps create together; here singers, dancers, and mimers, perhaps recruited from the young people, should be trained, and here from time to time also the children could be gathered to learn hymns and liturgical actions and be prepared for roles in special enactments.

Utopian?

All these proposals will seem utopian, and perhaps it is time to repeat the acknowledgment that they very possibly are. But some defense can be made. First, for the restructuring of congregational life nothing needs to be done, or has been proposed here, beyond the ordinary capacity of men to reorganize their institutions, or beyond the talents of the people in the congregations—if once the religious conception of congregational life can be shaken. Second, the working church as it now lives is already very largely structured on these lines. There are in fact two church structures: an official organization which is increasingly empty of the real energies of the church, and an underground of casual groups, interdenominational projects, schools, student and professional groups, and the like, which carry the real life of the church in society. But so long as these two structures compete, a split is created between worship and teaching on the one hand and the work of love on the other which must in the end be disastrous.

VI. MISSION: NEW CHRISTIANITIES

Dare We Speak?

What of the mission of the church? What of "Go ye therefore into all nations . . ."? So long as we wholeheartedly conceived of ourselves as a religion in competition with other religions, all seemed clear. We had the best religion and the duty of bringing its benefits—whether heaven or hospitals—to those who yet lacked them. The twentieth century's agonies of missionary motivation have simply reflected the confusion of our religiosity. Those who now advocate that we refrain altogether from "proselyting" only carry the confusion to its extreme. They continue to regard Christianity as a religion, note that there can be no final criterion for establishing that one religion is so superior to another as to warrant conversion, and draw the conclusion.

We cannot, however, evade confessing Jesus not only to each other but also to those who cannot yet make the confession. The social structures in which we live embrace believers and unbelievers alike. It is in those structures that we all hear the voices which summon and exhort us to the future, that we hear what believers call a word of God. We hear God together—indeed, my unbelieving golf partner speaks him to me. Therefore, the conversation in which we together seek our destiny is one which always already embraces both believers and unbelievers.

Not every involvement with my fellow needs to become an explicit exchange in our joint talk of the destiny of life, but any can. If I am involved with my fellow in such a way that words like "destiny" or "lord" are at all appropriate between us, then my life is involved with his in such a way that the justification and point of my life depends in part on what he says to me, on the word he brings me, on his will and decision. Then either he himself is, for so much, the lord of my destiny or, if he serves some lord, that lord is mine also. Thus either I serve two lords, him or his and mine, or we have the same lord. If my neighbor and I so speak to each other that such talk is seemly at all, I cannot say to him ". . . is my destiny" without also saying ". . . is our destiny."

We may not enjoy the missionary enterprise. The passing of the old religious self-confidence removes extraneous supports and motivations and leaves us with our naked confession. Then it is revealed that we believers are, as is always the case, unbelievers also. We are not really sure of our confession and therefore, other supports being gone, wish to be modest and reserved about it. It may be that this hesitancy has its advantages, but let us be clear that any attempt to justify theoretically a general silence can never be more than a blunder of reasoning.

Insofar as the world is secularized, we should have no missionary qualms, for debunking the false religions is a mere act of elementary love to those enslaved by them. One who loses a false religion loses nothing of value. Nor are believers the only debunkers. But when it is a believer who does this debunking he exposes the false religions by talking of Jesus Christ— and this is already the missionary proclamation.

However, secularization is, and no doubt will be, very unevenly realized. It seems, indeed, to be a strictly Western phenomenon. If the great religions of the non-Western world are indeed passé, they do not seem to know it. Even that particularly pestilent religion of the West, "the bourgeois religiosity of the American middle-class white Protestant suburban residential parish," undoubtedly contains many residual elements of a genuine religion which are certainly in no hurry to give place to some variety of postreligious faith.

What does "telling the gospel" mean when my hearer already observes such a live non-Christian religion? Does the missionary proclamation of Jesus' unique lordship mean propaganda for one religion and against all others? If so, exactly how? For the devotee of a non-Christian religion, does confessing that "Jesus is Lord" mean adopting the Christian religion? By what right do we proselytize? Or do we?

It seems that our hypothesis that Christian faith is an anti-religious religion should give us some help with these questions. It should at least free us to acknowledge the validity of other religions as religions without falsely concluding that we have nothing to say to their devotees. Such a conclusion is false because believers do not simply bring a proposed substitute for old religion; we relativize *all* religion. We are, moreover, enabled to recognize that we too have a religion and that our meeting with other religions is indeed a kind of religious competition, without necessarily being bound to enforce the triumph of our own.

The Mission to the Religions

A religion is fundamentally a body of language, a way of speaking about the point of life. I am aware that a religion may be other things as well, but will regard this aspect as fundamental. I do this because I believe that the God whom all religions seek is a Word. This is obviously an avowedly inner-Christian and theological justification for treating this side of religions as fundamental.

Christian faith, too, is a religion. Let us work this out using "Jesus is Lord" as our formula of confession. This says that what happened with Jesus will be and so was a lord happening to us. Jesus enacted the event of someone being our lord—and this not in the sense that he imitated an event occurring elsewhere, perhaps in eternity before all time. The occurrences of Jesus' life were and will be the acts of someone living the role of our lord, of someone doing the business of ruling us. Therefore the story of Jesus is both the news that we have a lord and the explication of what "having a lord" means. Therefore also "Jesus is Lord" is unintelligible or pagan apart from the story of Jesus, for only the narration of what happened with Jesus gives "lord" its specific content as a confession of faith. If we analyze "Jesus is Lord" we will get: "Jesus is the one who . . . ," where what follows "who" is in part narrative from the New Testament. The final consequence is that "Jesus is Lord" can be explicated—should someone ask "What do you mean?"—only by such narrating and that it is true only if this narration is true.

Moreover, in narrating "the story of Jesus" we cannot refrain from telling about him as a religious phenomenon—for example, we have to talk of "the kingdom of Heaven," of "faith" as a mode of religious behavior, of his praying to the God of Abraham, and the like. This is because only as a religious phenomenon can he be the occurrence of someone acting as and being our lord, for at least since the fall, religion or the practiced absence thereof is what we do by way of having or lacking a final outcome of our lives, i.e., of being those who can have or lack a lord. We pick up the result of the previous paragraph and add to it: "Jesus is Lord" is explicable only by the narration of what happened with Jesus—in religious history. To confess "Jesus is Lord" is therefore to assert statements which in themselves must be regarded as assertions of Jewish and Christian religion.

Here is our problem: Confessing Jesus as lord means coming to speak the language of the Jewish and Christian religion. Demanding that other people become Christian in this sense is, however, just what we seem no longer to be able to do.

The solution to this impasse is found by asking: What *is* the language of the Christian religion? We only need put the question to realize that in the sense of a given entity, of "a language" such as might be defined by a particular wordbook which we could then somehow teach to people, there is no such thing. Lutheran and Pentecostalist missionaries do not speak the same language themselves—and as for the language of the Bible, none of us speaks it very well. The truth, of course, is that the language of Christian religion is not a thing but a tradition.

A tradition, a handing-on, of language subsists only as the event of actually doing the handing-on—i.e., as the event where one who belongs in the tradition seeks understanding with one who does not yet. A tradition subsists just as the tradition-event in which one who has learned to use certain concepts and con- structions does in fact use them—i.e., seeks mutual understand- ing with someone who has learned a different language. The issue of such an event will be new language, that language which the two find as they learn what each must do to communicate with the other. Thus a tradition of language subsists just as the event in which it grows and changes. The continuity, the self-identity, of an historically-given language is just the event in which, as one in the tradition seeks understanding with that other one to whom he now hearkens and speaks, the agreements which regulate the language he already has are questioned and revised so as to lead to new bonds of common apprehension, new language-creating agreements.

For the Christian to bring a member of another religion to speak the language of Christian religion and for one who is converted to confessing Jesus Christ to come to speak the language of Christian faith in order to make this confession, is, therefore, a creative act by both, the creation of a language which will be identical neither with Christian religious language as the believer previously used it nor with the previous language of the other religion. The linguistic event which occurs when a believer witnesses that Jesus is lord and is met with an answering confession, is not that the believer makes a Western Christian out of the new believer but rather that the two together create a new religion—which religion is, in the act of tradition, precisely the new birth of the Christian religion and of the non-Christian religion at once. If we wish to call this syncretism, very well, but then we must remember that Christianity as a religion has been syncretistic from its birth. As a religion, Christianity began as a sort of Jewish mystery religion, as a typical Hellenistic mixture of Greek and Oriental elements.

Thus, for example, the Western Christian talks of "forgiveness" or, these days, of "freedom from the past for the future." Is the language of philosophical Buddhism about "emptiness" functionally analogous or not? This is exactly what the Christian and the Buddhist must find out between them—and they will find it out by creating a new language born of their effort to make themselves understood to each other, a language in which they can speak *together* of *both* forgiveness and emptiness. It will be in this new language that the Buddhist will confess Jesus—if indeed he does come to make such a confession. What that new lan-

guage will be like cannot be predicted in advance of the event
of its birth—and surely not by a Western theologian sitting in
his study. It is conceivable that the confession of Christ should
make its way outside our culture as a religion or religions which
we should be quite unable to understand or even recognize as
Christian—apart from strenuous interpretive efforts, which
would in effect be our recapitulating of the linguistic event in
which these new ways of confessing were born.

How Far Can We Go?

The believer will insist on only one thing, that in a new religious language it will be possible to confess Jesus, if not as
"lord" then in some other way which he, as one who has in the
past confessed Jesus as "lord," now at this time honestly can fulfill. What criteria operate here?

The final criterion will be that the new confession be accept-
able to the one to whom it is addressed: Jesus himself. If there
is anything which any confession of Jesus must assume, it is that
he is not passé, that the new confession—this utterance in the
language of a new Christian religion—is a new response in an
unbroken conversation in which one partner will always be the
same Jesus. The main issue is whether he will accept what we
say as a proper address to him. This we will discover on that day
when our works will be tested for whether they be gold and
jewels or straw and stubble.

But this is not a criterion we can now use, and there must be
some such criterion also. For the announcement of final judgment clearly supposes that we are able to prepare for it, that we
have available ways of governing our works so that they will
stand. In the present context of the language-creating invasion
of the world of not-yet-Christian religion, what might these be?
I will mention three.

First, the believer must see to it that the act of new understanding, as which the tradition lives and in which new religious
insight and language are born, really occurs. To stay with our
example, it will not do simply to proclaim "Christ grants emptiness" on the theory that all religious values or words for

salvation can be preempted for him. Rather, the believer who speaks of "forgiveness" and the Buddhist who speaks of "emptiness" must labor with each other until they reach agreement on what they mean, though not necessarily on what in fact to affirm. This will be signaled by the achievement of new ways of speaking in which they speak together of *both* "forgiveness" and "emptiness."

Second, we have so far talked of the language-creating move into new religious territory only as the creation of something new. From the other side, however, this new creation is simply the life and growth of the old tradition in which the believer lives. For the believer, the old way of confessing Jesus and the new way which he finds in conversation with, let us say, Buddhism, are not two languages but one—his language, the sum of ways in which he can speak about Jesus. Therefore the believer can assess the adequacy of the new language to translate what he could say of Jesus in the old, just as one whose old language is English can, as he adds French to his language, assess the adequacy of his French to say what he can say in English. The believer must continue the language-creating conversation as long as there are sides of his confession which *he* can say which he cannot yet say *with* his new partner.

Third, there is one material criterion: A religious language adequate to the confession of Jesus must be one in which it is possible to remember Jesus, to do the kind of thing the New Testament gospels do. If I cannot remember Jesus I cannot confess Jesus, for "Jesus" is the name of a historical figure. This means that an adequate religious language must be a language in which the kind of talking we call historical recollection is possible—as it does not seem to be in, for example, the present religious language of some varieties of Hinduism and Buddhism.

Let us conclude by translating back from our talk about language to somewhat broader terms. Most of our puzzles about the relation of faith in Christ to other religions result from assuming that "Christ" and the "religions" are static entities whose relation we are to trace and/or manipulate. This is a false assumption. The object of faith is the man Jesus in the tradition about him. For their part, the religions are traditions and nothing else. And traditions subsist only as the events of their interaction—for to whom can I hand on what is given me except to a member of some other tradition?

Rather, the confession of Christ makes its way in the world of religions as a religion-destroying and religion-creating word. It is itself a religious tradition and so lives only as it is handed on, i.e., meets other religious traditions. In this meeting it both destroys old religion and creates new. It does this as every living religion does. But it also does it in the free and radical way proper to a religion which has no care to preserve its status quo as a religion, which is glad to be challenged and relativized and changed, which sees the creation of new religions precisely as its religious task.

One last remark: Our talk of "the believer" and his "partner" is only a model. The event we have been discussing is one of great complexity involving many people and long periods of time. We measure here in centuries. This should comfort us in our worry about how long it is taking for the "younger" churches to develop indigenous forms of worship and theology. It is true that no Origen of Oriental or African Christianity has yet appeared. But we should remember that the Origen of Western Christianity did not appear until two hundred years after the first contact of the gospel with our religiosity. Nor should we expect that the birth of a new Christian religion will ever occur except as a long struggle of the perversion and reformation of the gospel, just as it occurred with us.

VII. FAITH: RELIGION AGAINST ITSELF

If our previous discussions all add up to any one thing, perhaps it is to a particular concept of faith. We therefore now ask: What is faith?

Faith is religion against itself. It is the life of a religious man whose religion consists in repenting of being religious. Or it is the life of an irreligious man whose critique of religion somehow becomes the heart of his life, and comes to be directed to acquiring clearer understanding of such strangely religious matters as "God" or "destiny."

We say exactly the same thing if we say: Faith is being hooked on the story of Jesus. For the contingent fact—the fact that God is the particular God he is, the believer says—is that there exist no alternative "faiths," that it is this story and not another which is in fact so proclaimed as future as to call us to antireligious religion or religious antireligion. Only when the story of the crucified one is told as the future—i.e., only when it is said of a crucified one that he is risen—does a life open which finds its religious hope precisely in the bankruptcy of religion. There are plenty of religions to choose from. But only some of them, those about Jesus as risen, have the structure of faith. Jesus-as-future and faith belong together. This argument is not an attempt at coercing faith, for by no neutral criteria can we argue that faith is necessarily better than some other mode of life.

Faith as a Situation

Faith is religion against itself. Orthodox Protestant theology already knew this and put it by saying that it is only the object of faith which is decisive for the content of faithful life. Given the sentence "I believe in Jesus Christ," we can fully explain the meaning of the whole sentence by explaining only the last two words. As a religion, as my activity and experience of believing, faith is not "saving," for *what* I believe is in part exactly that my believing is "nothing worth," is ambiguous and indecisive. Let me try to elucidate this so: "Faith" is the name of a situation.

"Faith" is our name for finding ourselves in a particular situation and now having to live in it. It is our name for finding ourselves in the situation of having the gospel told to us and having to deal with what it says about us. Faith is the situation of being together with Jesus in one historical space for action and decision—which comes about in the usual way, by being told about him. Thus faith is a "gift," for while it is I who live in this situation, it is not my act that put me there but rather the act of someone else telling me the gospel. Thus faith is "saving," for our destiny is precisely to live roles in his action and decision of love, and faith is the happening of that. And thus "works" do not "save," for what I do in this situation, how I deal with its various factors, does not establish the fact of my being in it.

The home of faith is therefore worship, the occurrence of people telling the gospel to each other. The life of faith is speaking; it is witness to Jesus. The consciousness of faith is theology, thinking how to make this witness. The authenticity of faith is that I do in fact live my real physical and social life in it.

Whereupon we are back with our deeds, our speaking, our thinking: with our religion. We cannot escape religion; faith is indeed a religion. Yet, once again, as soon as we have said this we must immediately insist that faith is not our doing or speaking or thinking. Faith is not a set of opinions about God and things. Nor is it a set of attitudes, whether toward God, our fellows, or ourselves. Nor is it a set of feelings. Nor is it a set of overt behaviors. Nor is it any judicious combination of these.

The misunderstanding which these traditional negations attack is one that has devastated the church from its beginning; they attack the religious misunderstanding of faith. "We are saved by faith" is something the church has always said. But then faith itself has been interpreted as our performance, so that what "faith alone" often has come to mean is: Here is this long list of things God wants us to do. But we don't do all of them. So God has decided to let us off most of them if we will just do this one —have faith. Therewith we end with the exact opposite of what we set out to apprehend, we end with an especially religious— and phony—version of that "salvation by works" which the church has always claimed to abhor.

Faith is not any set of my ideas or feelings or deeds or attitudes. It is a situation for me to live in. Yet living is thinking and feeling and doing and hoping. To live in the situation of faith is therefore to think, feel, do, and hope in that situation. Moreover, faith is not a situation like a box is a situation; it is a word-situation, a situation of being addressed and called to respond, called to think and feel and act and plan. It is not a situation in which a stick or stone might be located. It is a situation of life— if I am put into it, I live.

Thus faith can never be described separately from life in faith. When I try to repeat or pass on the word which creates the situation of faith, when I try to describe the object of faith, I necessarily talk theologically, I form and express particular theological opinions. So also I cannot call myself or others to believe except by calling to actions, to specific actions. Any apprehension of what it is to believe will always be a description of specific opinions and actions, of a religion. Yet having said that, we must hasten to insist that we can neither identify any particular theologizing with thinking in faith, nor lay down in advance which specific actions are those which will be faithfulness in any particular situation. I cannot conclude from observation of what opinions are in fact held, or of what acts are in fact done, that I or anyone else is or is not in faith.

To believe is to choose and shape my life in response to the gospel; faith is life as a conversation with those who tell me of Jesus. What I say and do as my side of the conversation has definite content: I make assertions and decisions. Yet the conversation is faith and not something else only because of what is said *to* me, because of the gospel, which, moreover, is always the permission to live in spite of what I think and choose. The response of the gospel to my response to it always begins "Nevertheless..."

Therefore, as I live in faith I do indeed give my life a particular shape and pattern: I play a role in the story of Jesus—which means that I do indeed play a role. But that this role-playing is faith and not pretense depends only on the situation in which I play it. Nor can inferences be drawn from which particular role I play, from which particular pattern I give my life, to whether or not this role-playing is faith.

The Doubleness of Faith

Therefore faith is an endlessly ambiguous phenomenon. It is never identifiable as faith. If I examine my own life or someone else's, I can never come into position to say "Here is a believer." As a phenomenon, as a pattern of life, faith is not distinguishable from unbelief. Indeed, *in itself*, it is not different from unbelief. For that faith is faith—i.e., a being addressed by a promise of God—is not given by what it itself is as a way of living but solely by that promise. If I am so addressed, if I am taken up in conversation with the gospel, then I am—regardless of what particular utterances make up my side of the conversation. The gospel's reply to my utterances is in any case "Nevertheless ..." We are saved by *God,* and believing as an intellectual act is precisely knowing this. If I do not admit it, the fact is not changed. Thus it is quite as correct to say that we are saved by the God in whom we disbelieve as that we are saved by the God in whom we believe. We can very well be saved through our unbelief.

A life which was authentically and actively expressed in thoughts and actions and feelings which as a phenomenon we would have to label "unbelief," could precisely as such be a life lived in conversation with the story of the one thus rejected and so a life in the situation of faith. Simply *the fact that* Jesus is proclaimed to me by the church, provides an other in my historical space, provides a future to rejoice in or rebel against. Nothing remains to be done. If the proclamation is made to me, I can live for something, whether it is to accept or oppose this other; I can be single-minded, clear in my existence, conscious of my fate; I can identify myself—can, that is, be saved. In the Christ in whom I believe or disbelieve I can find singleness of action and purpose, I can find identity.

In this aspect, faith is a sort of abstract self-transcendence, a life for an other which is nevertheless independent of my attitudes or actions toward that other and even of my beliefs as to what that other is. It is thus a clarity without necessary content, a clarity that is not clarity *about* anything specific. It is a consciousness that is above all conscious that it cannot trust any of its identifications of *what* it is a consciousness of. It is a religiosity which is endlessly free to see through itself. In this aspect, faith is an abstract and ruthless honesty.

The honesty which is faith, in this aspect, is honesty which turns endlessly back on itself. In the grip of this honesty I see through every specific role I adopt, I debunk every label I hang on myself, every claim to be a believer or an unbeliever or a patriot or a liberal or what will you, and then I next debunk also the negation of the claim. I am free from needing to make such claims at all. In this honesty, I have identity and singleness as a person exactly in finding out and admitting the questionableness and pretense of every identification I give myself, every part I play. I am my true self exactly in confessing that all my works are ambiguous and unreliable, that every interpretation I give my life—as a life of virtue, or power, or humility, or normality, or rebellion—can be immediately replaced by an opposed interpretation which will be equally true, and so on indefinitely.

Faith in this aspect has not remained the monopoly of Christians. Rather, it has become a specific mark of contemporary culture: the corrosive Nietzschean honesty which can see through everything, the infinite reflection which can always discover yet another side to every question. The result of such honesty is that all reality becomes ambiguous, all happenings become capable of an infinity of successive interpretations. We come to live in a world in which nothing is firm and reliable, where every opinion may be overthrown momentarily, where every course of action may lead to the opposite of the intended result—if it really was intended! We come to live in a world which offers no security. These are very modern themes, but their discoverers were Luther, who could not tell God from the devil or faith from blasphemy; Søren Kierkegaard, who taught us the endlessness of reflection on what we are to live for; and the man who first said, "Lord, I believe. Help thou my unbelief!"

Yet this radical honesty which is faith can never be by itself. It arises precisely as my playing a role in the story of Jesus, and even though it then turns on and debunks the significance of that role-playing insofar as it is something *I* do, it does not simply terminate it, being itself real only as this critique. Also in its secularized form, radical honesty can never be the whole of life, for even though I see through every role I adopt, I must play some role or my life will have no plot and there will be no I to do this seeing-through. I necessarily have to be some particular thing, I have to enact some specific story, I have to have determinate opinions about and attitudes toward the other or others over against whom I live. Life can never be abstract honesty alone.

Thus my life as a believer is at once radical honesty, a life-for-someone which is independent of what I do or think in so living, and the role-playing, the concrete doing and thinking, which is my living this life. To be a believer is to play a concrete part in the story of Jesus—this is faith in its second aspect.

This role-playing is utterly unsupernatural. It is simply that as I make my daily choices and reckonings, I reckon with Jesus and what, on the basis of past performance in Palestine, he will say, just as I reckon with what my family, friends, and associates have said and will say. I reckon with a final address to me that will rehearse for me the meaning-as-love of the deed which I am doing or contemplating doing.

Faith, in this aspect as role-playing, is earthly. It is playing a role in Jesus' story in the "body," with the events of our lives here and now—not in the proud consciousness we have just spoken of, the proud consciousness by which we transcend ourselves. It is a sort of secular mysticism, an identification with

Jesus which posits no mysterious common spirit-substance between him and us, but only the ordinary reality of history, the
network of language, by which the stories of many lives come to
make one story together. It may also involve—and perhaps
usually will—the psychic mechanisms of projection and interior-
ization with which we are so familiar. It may very well involve
projections and interiorizations which are "abnormal"—which
need not distress us at all.

The unbeliever too must play some role in life. If he is one
caught up in the worldliness of our time, he will be aware, with
the same Nietzschean honesty as the believer, of the fact that
he is playing a role. So what is the difference between believer
and unbeliever? Merely that the believer plays the role of par-
ticipant in Jesus' story and the unbeliever plays some other?
Exactly. But the "merely" is inappropriate. For unless the history
in which I play my role is the history of a crucified and risen
one, role-playing and radical honesty are disconnected from each
other. I simply see through all my concrete deeds and thoughts
in life, see through the role I play—and that is all. If I then seek
a new role or persist in the old one, it is not because I have any
answer to my self-critique, but only because I cannot help it,
because I cannot stop role-playing except by ceasing to live. In
this division between life and self-transcendence, I am tempted
either to assert my role stubbornly against all critique and become an ideologist, or to push through my honesty at the cost of
never doing anything specific. Both outcomes are familiar
phenomena of our culture. We all know the ideologist who does
indeed know what it would be to be honest with himself and has
closed his mind exactly to avoid this. We also know the bitterly
honest seeker unable to find any role to play and so immobilized
by his honesty. Most of us survive more comfortably than these
two opposite sorts of radicals only because we incoherently mix
together a bit of each of their sorts of damnation.

Why should it be different if my role is that of fellowman of
Jesus? Jesus was one the act of whose life was precisely the love
of "sinners," of those who did not and did not want to love him in
return. When therefore I see through and debunk my playing

the role of one who follows him, when I unmask it in myself as pretense and custom and hypocrisy, this does not disqualify me in my role. It confirms me in it. Exactly his phony followers are the ones he certifies as his own. Jesus was a crucified one, he "died for us." That is, the very conclusion of the act of love which was his life was at the same time the conclusion of the hatred or indifference for him of those whom he loved. When his story is proclaimed to us as our future, so that we are included among those he loved, nothing, therefore, can exclude us from his love, not even all the ungodliness that the radical honesty of faith itself can discover in us. To turn back for a moment to the language of the doctrine of God: God exists for us precisely as the event of being rejected by us. He is therefore irrevocably ours.

Faith is both concrete life as historical and psychological involvement with Jesus of Nazareth and radically honest critique of all concrete life. If we substitute any other name for "Jesus," we will get a general description of the existence of contemporary man, in all the glory and malaise of his inner dividedness. The believer's life is no less divided in itself, yet *for* him the division is overcome, for the other toward whom he transcends himself is identified for him, by the proclamation that Jesus is risen and is coming again, as one whose story he knows and with whose story he can therefore become concretely involved. Vice versa, vital concrete involvement with this man of the past is possible at all only because this proclamation, the gospel, tells that he is risen and so promises him as our final future. Thus it is the word that Jesus is risen, the word that a man of the past will be our last future, that unites the believer's life, that unites past and future, role-playing and free self-transcendence. Yet this word would only intensify the inner incoherence between role-playing and self-transcendence were it not that it is a crucified one who is said to be risen and coming—so that even by the most destructive radical honesty we cannot separate ourselves from him. Indeed, it is only because the believer lives for the crucified one who loves him no matter what, that his self-transcendence is independent of any particular attitudes or opinions, that it is radical honesty. There is a model for this description of faith: Klara in Olav Hartmann's *Holy Masquerade*.

Thus the unity of faith as a way of life occurs as someone saying to the believer, "The crucified is risen and will come." It does not occur in what the believer does and suffers but rather as the unity of *Jesus'* life, as the occurrence of crucifixion and resurrection as events in the one life of this one person. The unity of the life of faith is not the achievement of the believer; it is the achievement of Jesus Christ, who succeeded in being one person as both crucified and risen by suffering his death without losing the love that was fulfilled in the resurrection.

One last step: The unity of faith as a way of life is therefore something promised to the believer, something he awaits from the future. For to say of Jesus that he is crucified and risen is to say that he is crucified and will come. "He is risen" is a prophecy: the prophecy that he will be our last future. The believer will receive the unity and singleness of his life when—and if— the Jesus of Nazareth on whose story he is hooked does indeed come on the day dated by death to settle our destinies. The believer will receive the unity of his life when and if the historical figure around whose story he plays his role and the future lord toward whom he transcends himself in radical freedom and honesty do indeed prove to be the same.

Faith may therefore be called hopeful double-mindedness. It is a divided life lived, as such, by the promise that the division will be overcome.

Faith as the Ordinary

Therefore faith is simply the hopeful version of human life as all men live it, made hopeful by the story about Jesus. If in our time we describe faith as a hopeful life of inner division, it is as inner division that the gospel has taught us in our time to see and live all human life. Faith is not a supernatural accomplishment, or a gift of infused spirit-substance from above. It is the gift of human life. And it is a gift from here below, where the Christian God happens, a gift of people talking and enacting with each other the tale of Jesus. Grace is simply the hopeful version of nature.

This is why faith is an ambiguous phenomenon. The man of faith does nothing special. In his politics and work, he does what men of good will do. In his "private" life, he tries to be loving and faithful. He is, perhaps somewhat apologetically, religious. He does, to be sure, gather with others to indulge in the decidedly odd activity of carrying on about Jesus. But this can always be interpreted on the model of a religious society, and the believer will be the first to make this interpretation, so far as the praying, singing, etc., are things *he* does.

The believer does the ordinary business of life. The only thing is—he does it.

Faith as we have described it is not a new kind of "worldly" faith for our worldly age. Our worship, our theology, our ethics, and our witness will and must change with the progress of the gospel through history. The life of faith changes, and since faith cannot be described separately from life in faith, with it our description of faith will change—this description is after all a part of theology. But as the situation of being in this history, faith itself will be always the same. What we have said here of faith has always been true of faith—but it takes what the gospel teaches us in our time to discover it.

Faith is worldly existence. It is religion against itself. That is why, in the age when we see this, the program of antireligious worship, theology, and life is possible and required—or so it seems to those of us Christians who repent our own religiosity.

VIII. HOMILETICAL ATTEMPTS

The proof of any theology is in the preaching. Indeed, it is not possible fully to understand a theology apart from hearing—or, if necessary, reading—some of the preaching associated with it. For theology is but thinking through how to get the gospel said; i.e., theology is thinking about what is to be said in preaching.

To preach is simply to tell the story of Jesus as gospel. It is promising people Jesus of Nazareth as their future. It can therefore occur anywhere that the subject can come up. All preaching, however, has its center in that preaching which is a liturgical act, which occurs as part of the enactment of the preached events. This may be a formal sermon, or it may not. Yet once over the first intoxication of freedom from the ways of our fathers, we probably will find few better forms. There is nothing particularly the matter with the sermon as a way of preaching; dissatisfaction with it is probably the result not of the form but of the preacher's not having anything to say worth taking so long about.

The purpose of this chapter is not to discuss the problems of preaching, but to come to one point of the previous chapters by doing what they demand—or rather, that of what they demand that can be done in a book at all.

The very short sermons which follow are not printed as examples of how to preach. No claims are made for their quality or effectiveness. They are some attempts to narrate the story of Jesus and our stories as one story together, by narrating Jesus' story as future. They appear only as samples of what this might sound like, only as a necessary part of what this book tries to say. Originally, all were preached in the chapel of Luther College at

Decorah, Iowa. The marks of their address to a student congregation have been left; all true preaching is addressed to some particular congregation.

SOME WEEKS AFTER THE ASSASSINATION OF JOHN F. KENNEDY

> "But in fact Christ has been raised from the dead, the first fruits of those who have fallen asleep. For as by a man came death, by a man has come also the resurrection of the dead. For as in Adam all die, so also in Christ shall all be made alive." (1 Corinthians 15:20-22.)

Perhaps enough time is now past to begin *reflection* on the event of John Kennedy's assassination. I begin with personal reflection.

For me and for at least some others, the assassination was an interruption in our own lives, a dead-end in life from which we too have had to make a kind of fresh start. Something terrible happened to us also—we *had* to have the caisson and the riderless horse and Charles de Gaulle to give form and stability to our disturbance. Otherwise we could not have contained it.

What *was* that disturbance? How are we to explain the urgency and totality of the shock?

I believe that John Kennedy, whatever reservations about his policies we may have had, symbolized *hope*. He was self-consciously of the post-World War II generation; he had broken with many of the old ideologies; he was committed to exactly those causes in which the *future* may be hidden. We hoped that whatever he would finally accomplish, at least it would not be more only of the same old stuff. Perhaps we were deluded in hoping this. But we did.

And then in one instant all those possibilities hidden in him were canceled. Hope met death—and death triumphed.

The death of John Kennedy was, for some of us at least, a uniquely insistent revelation of the mystery of man. Man lives by hope—he lives by what he *will* do, *will* become, *will* create. He lives, if you will, by dreaming. And yet man the dreamer's one certain future is death—which turns possibility into might-have-been. The paradox of possibility and death is the paradox of man. The crumpled young Caesar was an image of that paradox almost too clear to be borne.

The sudden intrusion of that image was what stopped, for a time, our usual ways.

At some few times, one's theology undergoes a drastic concentration. Under the impact of that image, my theology reduces to this:

I am left with a demand inside that all this of our loving and fighting and thinking and suffering and eating and making not be in vain, that this magnificent but unfinished story of ours not just break off, that possibility be redeemed.

And I am left with an inability to escape from what I have heard about Jesus of Nazareth. In his life this mystery of man seems to have received its final enactment. He preached the Kingdom of God, the day when all the possibility which flickers in our lives would be realized—and he was killed on account of it.

And I am left with this claim I have heard, this news that has been brought—that he is risen—that the mystery of man, the mystery of possibility and death, is *somehow* a mystery of light and not of darkness, of hope and not of uselessness.

And I am left with God—who is, then, simply the object of my demand and the speaker of that claim—and of whom we need know no more.

For the rest, perhaps we ought not be too easily comforted. When a man dies young, there is a whole human future which now only might have been—until that day when all might-have-beens will be opened to us as the true future of God and man. But that is not *easy* comfort. That is death and resurrection.

SHORTLY BEFORE CHRISTMAS

It is about time for various religious leaders and such to begin denouncing the commercialism of Christmas. Probably this needs to be done occasionally, and I may even join in later. But if past experience is a guide, sooner or later one of them will attack fancy gift wrappings and "Jingle Bells" and Santa Claus—and then I draw the line.

What, after all, is the matter with these things? They are "secular"; they are not religious enough. And somehow the opinion circulates that in order to be *real* Christians we have to live always by reference to the ultimate issues—whether "heaven" or the social revolution.

Moreover, they are not serious enough. And life, say the religious, is a serious matter—even when it is admitted that it should be leavened with that grimmest of affairs, "good Christian fun." Thus at Christmas we must reflect always on the discomforts of the stable, the sinfulness of the innkeepers, and the ultimate bitter destiny of the babe.

Do not mistake me. We indeed live every act of our lives in the presence of God. But if we find no place in the life of faith for "Jingle Bells," if we sing such joyous things as Britten's "Ceremony of Carols" at concerts but not in church, or if we sing the same carol gaily and spontaneously outside a girls' dormitory at midnight and glumly and lugubriously in chapel, then we have misunderstood which God we are dealing with. For the real God before whom we live, the God of Christmas, is not nearly so religious and serious as we are. He does not only enjoy hymns. He likes to relax a little from time to time.

The word from God for this morning is "Merry Christmas." A baby has lived and defined the life of God. Babies laugh and giggle—which means *God* laughs and even giggles. And who can be religious while changing diapers?

It is time to sing for the fun of it, time to decorate windows, to be materialistic and tell your beloved that you would love a useless negligee. It is time to sing bouncy tunes in church, and some evenings not study very hard—with a clear conscience.

For our judge will be one who has let down to the enormous extent of playing in the Palestinian equivalent of sandboxes and such—who has endorsed the childish side of life

PSALM 22

In the centuries before Christ it happened no doubt many times that a man, clad in rags of sorrow, entered the great tem-

ple in Jerusalem, stood up in the gathering of worshipers, and
reading the great text from memory, with perhaps his own personal additions, prayed:

> My God, my God, why hast thou forsaken me?
>> Why art thou so far from helping me, from the words of my
>> groaning?
> O my God, I cry by day, but thou dost not answer;
>> and by night, but find no rest.
>
> Yet thou art holy,
>> enthroned on the praises of Israel.
> In thee our fathers trusted;
>> they trusted, and thou didst deliver them.
> To thee they cried, and were saved;
>> in thee they trusted, and were not disappointed.
>
> But I am a worm, and no man;
>> scorned by men, and despised by the people
> All who see me mock at me,
>> they make mouths at me, they wag their heads;
> "He committed his cause to the Lord; let him deliver him,
>> let him rescue him, for he delights in him!"
>
> Yet thou art he who took me from the womb;
>> thou didst keep me safe upon my mother's breasts
> Upon thee was I cast from my birth,
>> and since my mother bore me thou hast been my God.
> Be not far from me,
>> for trouble is near
>> and there is none to help.
>
> Many bulls encompass me,
>> strong bulls of Bashan surround me;
> they open wide their mouths at me,
>> like a ravening and roaring lion.
>
> I am poured out like water,
>> and all my bones are out of joint;
> my heart is like wax,

it is melted within my breast;
my strength is dried up like a potsherd,
   and my tongue cleaves to my jaws;
   thou dost lay me in the dust of death.

Yea, dogs are round about me;
   a company of evildoers encircle me;
   they have pierced my hands and feet—
I can count all my bones—
   they stare and gloat over me;
they divide my garments among them,
   and for my raiment they cast lots.

But thou, O Lord, be not far off!
   O thou my help, hasten to my aid!
Deliver my soul from the sword,
   my life from the power of the dog!
Save me from the mouth of the lion,
   my afflicted soul from the horns of the wild oxen!

                                              (Psalm 22:1-21.)

Then followed the waiting—for a few minutes, a day, twenty years, what did it matter?—for the prophet speaking in the name of the Lord to pronounce the healing assurance. Then came the cry, in verse 21, "He has heard me!" And then came the great thanksgiving hymn of the last verses—but it is too soon to go on to them.

Why was he there, this petitioner? What experience had driven him to the temple? Sickness, as it seems, sent by the witchcraft of his enemies. Yet it is plain that his sickness and the guile of his enemies were for him but signs of the real cause of his pain—*the silence of God.* He had tried to pray, had tried to sing hymns, had tried to call forth that Word of God which everyone else talked of hearing—and had been able to hear nothing at all. God had deserted him. For him, at least, God just was not there.

Our problem is deeper than any mere skepticism. Our fathers trusted in God. They believed he worked things out in their lives, that he spoke to them and guided them. Nor is there any good reason to doubt them, to dispute whether God exists. We were brought up in that security. And we seem to remember that once God was real for us. But now it just couldn't matter less. Probably there is a God and probably he spoke to our fathers—but he doesn't speak to us.

And so we believe in a fashion. We reckon with a distant, abstract Great Force or Cosmic Love of some sort. But he is indeed distant and abstract—and useless. He provides no hand of comfort in the large and small crises of our lives. The preachers speak much *about* "the gospel" but do not seem ever to be able to speak *it*. At least we do not hear it.

Our experience of God is the experience precisely of his *silence*.

Here some flee to a bottle or a stick. Others of you will flee to the phony religion of "Love" or Sweet Jesus or the Christian Anti-Communism Crusade. More of us will turn merely to a dull disinterest in life from which, after it has lasted awhile, not all the liberal arts nor yet Gabriel's trump will be able to waken us.

But this one in the temple—he did something astonishing. He fled exactly to the Silent God. If God would not speak, if he would remain strange and distant and cold, why then he would cling exactly to God's Silence and *so* hold to him!

If it is his silence God gives us, that is much. That we hear his absence is to hear him. And though it may seem little to have of God, it is all Jesus of Nazareth had at the end—and it sufficed.

If God is silent, we may cling to his silence. We may pray and sing to his silence. We may work for our fellows in common knowledge of what we all together lack of security and religious confidence. We may live trusting to his silence.

How long may a silence of God last? Who knows? And what difference can it make? Ten seconds is plenty, and a lifetime no worse.

For now—

Let us simply rejoice that God lets us hear at least his silence—to prepare us for the day when we and all the generations of those who have prayed, whether in vehemence or resignation, "O my God, I cry by day, but thou dost not answer; and by night, but find no rest," will hear the prophet Jesus speak from the door of the temple and responding join in the hymn with which the psalm concludes, the hymn chanted before the crowd in the temple by one who had prayed the prayer of abandonment, waited—and at last heard God speak:

> I will tell of thy name to my brethren;
>   in the midst of the congregation I will praise thee:
> You who fear the Lord, praise him!
>   all you sons of Jacob, glorify him,
>   and stand in awe of him, all you sons of Israel!
> For he has not despised or abhorred
>   the affliction of the afflicted;
> and he has not hid his face from him,
>   but has heard, when he cried to him.
>
> From thee comes my praise in the great congregation;
>   my vows I will pay before those who fear him.
> The afflicted shall eat and be satisfied;
>   those who seek him shall praise the Lord!
>   May your hearts live for ever!
>
> All the ends of the earth shall remember
>   and turn to the Lord;
> and all the families of the nations
>   shall worship before him.
> For dominion belongs to the Lord,
>   and he rules over the nations.
>
> Yea, to him shall all the proud of the earth bow down;
>   before him shall bow all who go down to the dust,
>   and he who cannot keep himself alive.
> Posterity shall serve him;
>   men shall tell of the Lord to the coming generation,
> and proclaim his deliverance to a people yet unborn,
>   that he has wrought it.
>
> (Psalm 22:22-31.)

ACTS 3:1-16

A couple of nights ago it was seven-year-old Kari's turn to read the Bible. More or less at random I gave her this passage to read:

> "Now Peter and John were going up to the temple at the
> hour of prayer, the ninth hour. And a man lame from birth was
> being carried, whom they laid daily at that gate of the temple
> which is called Beautiful to ask alms of those who entered
> the temple. Seeing Peter and John about to go into the tem-
> ple, he asked for alms. And Peter directed his gaze at him,
> with John, and said, 'Look at us.' And he fixed his attention
> upon them, expecting to receive something from them. But
> Peter said, 'I have no silver and gold, but I give you what I
> have; in the name of Jesus Christ of Nazareth, walk.' And he
> took him by the right hand and raised him up; and immediately
> his feet and ankles were made strong." (Acts 3:1-7.)

At this point she stopped and exclaimed, "He could do it too!"
We talked, and she saw immediately that the point of Peter's
being able to do it too was to turn attention to Jesus, as shown
by the way the story leads up to a sermon:

> "While he clung to Peter and John, all the people ran together
> to them in the portico called Solomon's, astounded. And when
> Peter saw it he addressed the people, 'Men of Israel, why
> do you wonder at this, or why do you stare at us, as though
> by our own power or piety we had made him walk? The God of
> Abraham and of Isaac and of Jacob, the God of our fathers,
> glorified his servant Jesus, whom you delivered up and denied
> in the presence of Pilate, when he had decided to release him.
> But you denied the Holy and Righteous One, and asked for a
> murderer to be granted to you, and killed the Author of life,
> whom God raised from the dead. To this we are witnesses.
> And his name, by faith in his name, has made this man strong
> whom you see and know; and the faith which is through Jesus
> has given the man this perfect health in the presence of you all.'"
> (Acts 3:11-16.)

Jesus' disciples could do it too! Do what? Tell cripples to walk
and see them do so? Maybe. Why not? But had I been ill even
then, I would have looked up a doctor—there were many sick
and, as the Bible says, only a few were miraculously healed. Nor
did the apostles set up shop as faith-healers. What their healing
meant is apparent from the continuation of the text: it was an
acting out of the Resurrection, of what they had to tell about; an

acting out that one man, Jesus, had established that death and suffering are not the last word about human life.

Jesus' disciples—we, that is—can do it too. Do what? Let me put it this way: *act against the probabilities,* to demonstrate what Jesus did; act against the probabilities for the sake of life.

On everything in life, we can reckon up the odds. Thinking of marriage, we can hit off the relevant factors—family, religion, education, sex appeal, age, emotional stability, etc.—and then make an estimate of the chances of success. Peter could have worked out the chances of the cripple's ever walking again. We can canvass the likelihood of our social revolution under Negro auspices breaking down fixed structures of behavior. Offered a job, I want to know the probabilities of advancement.

Quite clearly, it belongs to security and decency to make such reckonings. But it belongs to *life* sometimes not to act on them. It belongs to life sometimes to take the job with no visible future because it is what you, irrationally enough, want to do; to marry the fellow in spite of the dismal predictions of your friends; to enroll in a quixotic crusade. For the probabilities are the dead hand of the past on the future. They predict how things *will* go on the basis of how they *have* gone. And to regulate one's life always by the probabilities is to give in to death ahead of time.

That is, of course, what we mostly do. You can do it by conforming—most of you will take a safe position, marry someone very like yourselves, and spend your lives keeping your noses clean. Or you can do it by rebelling—with the cynic's very careful assessment of the low chances that people will prove trustworthy and of the rarity of goodness in society as it is, and with the cynic's very calculating regulation of his life by these estimates.

Jesus of Nazareth lived differently. His life was one long defiance of what everybody knew for sure. He preached of the surprises God had for the despairing and the confident alike, about "forgiveness." He made his friends among those for whom statistically there was little hope. This too was the meaning of his healings: they were tokens against the probability of disease and death.

And at last he bet his life and work on the tremendous improbability that death would not be the conclusion.

You can do it too. To be sure, sober realism in assessing reality as it is is one of Christian faith's oft-touted virtues. And we must indeed weigh and balance and be realistic. Yet to Christian faith there also belongs a kind of innocent optimism, which may be hard to feel but by which we can act anyway, which—not always, but sometimes—acts against the odds and bets on the long-shot, which can say to a cripple "Stand up," or to an entrenched injustice "Down with it," or to a risky career "Let's try it"—for the sake of life itself.

For the sake of life as Jesus has defined it, we can throw ourselves into the glad creativity and despairing struggle of life in our great cities with hope and disillusion. We can carry our sign or write our letter or speak up in a committee always expecting our unimpressive voice may be the one that is heard.

Such cheerful wrongheadedness acts out in our lives Jesus' long-shot bet on us, his overturning of the known figures on sinners repenting and sick men recovering and the dead rising.

You can do it too. What is to stop you? For the story of Jesus' Resurrection is the message that the future is, after all, on the side of the risk-takers.